If It Had Not Been for the Lord

Captured by His Love and Kept by His Grace

Rev. Dr. Theresa Chatman

PUBLISHED BY
OUR WRITTEN LIVES OF HOPE, LLC

Our Written Lives of Hope provides publishing services for authors in various educational, religious, and human service organizations. For information, visit www.OurWrittenLives.com.

Copyright ©2017 Theresa Chatman
Interior Designed by Our Written Lives

Library of Congress Cataloging-in-Publication Data
Theresa Chatman 1968–
If It Had Not Been for the Lord:
Captured by His Love and Kept by His Grace

Library of Congress Control Number: 2017954658
ISBN: 978-1-942923-27-5 (paperback)

If It Had Not Been for the Lord

Captured by His Love and Kept by His Grace

Dedication

First, I wish to dedicate this book to my Lord and Savior Jesus Christ. I know without Him, I could do nothing.

Secondly, I wish to dedicate this book to my husband, James, who understands me and accepts me for who I am. Thank you for your never-ending love, support, and patience throughout this book writing project.

Forward

Let the fire of God within you shine! Light has an impact. When we walk in a room, our light—God's fire or anointing—should cause a shift in the atmosphere. Our presence has the power to pierce the darkness because we are the light of the world, or the fire of the world.

There will come a time when men will hate us because of the light that is in us. As God begins using us in a miraculous way, the more we will be hated without a cause. The fire of God empowers us to love others in spite of the way they treat us.

The love of God compels us to forgive people that use us and diminish the presence of God within us God has manifested His love in our lives, so we can show the same love to others. Keep loving! Keep forgiving! Love covers a multitude of sins. Love looks beyond the flaws of others and sees the frail state of the man.

Isaiah 53:3 says, "He is despised and rejected by men, a man of sorrows and acquainted with grief. And we hid, as it were, our faces from Him; He was despised, and we did not esteem Him." If Jesus went through all of that, what do you think we will go through?

In this book, I share my story of times when people hated me, mistreated me, and abused me. God's love kept me through it all, and God always provided someone to help me through. At the end of each chapter, I share questions for you to ask yourself. Think deeply on each question, and allow God to reveal His purpose for your story.

Contents

1: The Power of Thought _____ 11

2: The Heart of a Child _____ 19

3: An Identity Free of Shame_____ 29

4: A Prosperous Life_____ 37

5: Rebuilding Trust _____ 49

6: From Insecurity to Success _____ 55

7: Chains are Broken _____ 63

8: Jealousy _____ 73

9: Relinquishing Control _____ 81

10: Tragedy Struck at Midnight _____ 87

11: From Fear to Faith_____ 99

12: Flawed, but Called _____107

13: Alright_____115

About the Author _____126

chapter 1
The Power of Thought

Death and life are in the power of the tongue . . .
Proverbs 18:21 KJV

Our thoughts are powerful; they determine the direction we take, our actions, and experience of life. The best thing about the power of our thoughts is the fact that God gives us authority over our thoughts. We own our thoughts, and we have the authority to direct them. The mind will go where we allow it to go. We can steer our minds toward the direction we choose. Whatever we decide to think about will influence our lives. We must train our minds to obey our will.

Taking authority over our thoughts isn't always easy. The challenge comes when we encounter our built-up history of self-defeating ideas. Negative thoughts come from a variety of external forces: our parents, siblings, other family members, strangers, teachers, friends, television, and more. We possess the power to adopt or reject each belief we encounter.

The Word of God is the one influence always working for the good of those who allow it to saturate their spirit. God's Word will not return void. God will fulfill every promise ordained in His Word. The scriptures reinforce the important benefit and urgent need to meditate on what is good, pure, and honest.

As beneficial as it is to focus on God's Word and the positives of life, it is easier for us to believe negativity and lies over believing God's Truth. It is God's will for believers to take hold of the Truth and replace old thought patterns. Success happens when we act on the Truth and reject the lies the enemy of our destiny has told us.

Throughout this book, I will share areas of my life where I had to take authority over negative thinking and turn it around to align with the Truth of God's Word. In each chapter, I'll share a small story of my life, how I overcame the challenge I was facing, the life lesson I learned, and how you can apply the lesson I learned to your life. As I share my story, think about your life, your thoughts, and your emotions. Begin to replace any lies with God's Truth.

My Thoughts and My Identity

I once read that my name, Theresa, means "diligent harvester." Since that time, I took my name's meaning seriously and set my heart and mind to be a hard worker in everything I did. Work was a central part of my life. I was faithful and completed work effectively and efficiently. I carried my work ethic into any endeavor I put my hands forward to do. I believed I was a "diligent harvester." My belief impacted my character and the energy I put forth.

Chapter 1 • The Power of Thought

One of my first jobs was working at a restaurant. I worked my way all the way up to crew chief, learning everything there was to know from front counter duties to the back of the kitchen. I could fire up and use the grill, make salads and biscuits, man the drive-through, and work the cash register. I could do it all. I was driven to succeed, even in the small things. Faithfulness to that job taught me the importance of hard work, diligence, and customer service.

No matter what I did, I did it with all my heart, as unto the LORD. The Bible says when we serve the Lord with all we are, He will reward us. There is no way but up for the faithful worker. Showing up every day with the intention of giving my best was the truest trait of success. There was no failure in putting forth a committed effort to do my best, and it all began with one affirming thought about myself. "I am a diligent harvester."

I applied the same mode of thought I held about my work into ministry for the Lord. I examined my motivation toward service and committed myself to God's call on my life. I wanted everything I did to be pure and founded on love. I wanted my love for God to be first, and for His love to flow through me to others.

No matter how loving, diligent, and hardworking I have been, I've had times where I felt unappreciated and used. Some people viewed my kindness as weakness, critiquing my work, or taking credit for the things I did. I would overlook their rudeness for a time, trying to focus on the positive, but when I couldn't take the disrespect anymore, my thoughts turned negative.

That's when the not-so-kind side of me would rear its ugly head. I am not at all proud of my ugly side because it has pushed many people away. People never expected ugliness from me, but it was there under the surface nonetheless. Even on my wedding day, someone took a picture of me that captured a look of deep sadness on my face. The sadness I felt was a result of a painful thought crossing my mind.

My thoughts have led me to every decision I have made. Some of my choices were terrific, while others were self-destructive. My thoughts can bring me down into fear, dread, and regret. Oh, yes, a lot of regret. It is only by God's mercy my thoughts did not drive me to commit life-threatening behaviors. Some of the life choices I made have left me with tremendous emotional baggage, but I have survived to write about it all.

Merriam-Webster's contemporary definition of the word *thought* is: "ideas or opinions produced by thinking or occurring suddenly in the mind." If it is true that ideas, opinions, and thoughts occur "suddenly," it stands to reason that one has no control over all the thoughts of the mind. It is true, some thoughts do appear suddenly, uninvited and against our will. But we do have total control over the dominant thought that rules our minds.

It's our job to cast down any thought that is contrary to the will of God. According to 2 Corinthians 10:5, "We demolish arguments and every pretension that sets itself up against the knowledge of God, and we take captive every thought to make it obedient to Christ." When the Word of God dominates our thoughts, every other unwelcome, negative thought holds no power. We can align our thoughts with God's Word.

I Have Overcome

As I look back over my life and all God has taught me, I see many transformations. I look at the person I am now compared to the person I was, particularly in terms of my thought life. There were times in the past when negative thoughts controlled me. My thoughts would determine if I was happy or sad, up or down. When negative thoughts of past events and experiences would cross my mind, my disposition would change spontaneously.

Comparatively, today I have learned to not allow my thoughts to control me. I see my thoughts for what they are—fleeting moments—and not the reality of who I am. I allow negative thoughts to pass through my mind like a dark cloud, while I aim to look for the coming sunlight.

In this human experience, everyone will have cloudy thoughts that try to block out the reality of hope and truth. I had to learn the power of controlling my thoughts and not allowing negativity to drain my well of positive thinking. I have a wealth of Truth stored inside of me, and I tapped into the positive side of my thought reservoir.

Galatians 5:22-23 says it best, "But the fruit of the Spirit is love, joy, peace, longsuffering, gentleness, goodness, faith, meekness, temperance, against such there is no law." When I allowed God to take charge of my thoughts, the Holy Spirit began to manifest in my mind. My character and purpose come from the Spirit of God as I surrender my thoughts to His will.

We all want to live to our full potential, and that journey begins with our thoughts. The more we discover the innate purpose for which we were born, the more we can move closer to fulfilling our potential. I refuse to believe I have reached as high as I can go. I refuse to settle for less than my God-given potential.

As a human, my first innate purpose is to worship my Creator. He designed me, intricately weaving intelligence throughout my personality. He is the one who made me into a sensitive and altruistic person. He has made me who I am, and I am good. When I truly believe God created me for a purpose, I won't embody the disposition of a doormat. Instead, I will walk upright, believing I am somebody, I belong, and I can do all things through Christ.

Lesson Learned

Life is the compilation of one decision that dominoes into the next decision. The mind and its thoughts play a major role in mobilizing us forward and upward. Every day is a process of renewing and working on the inward person, bringing all thoughts captive to Christ.

Chapter 1 • The Power of Thought | 17

I've learned that destiny is wrapped up, tangled up, and hinged upon what I chose to think and to believe. If I believe a lie, I will live a lie. If I believe God, I will live by the power of His sustaining Holy Spirit. Any position, title, educational degree, worldly accolade or recognition means nothing without belief in the King of kings and the Lord of lords. I can do nothing without God in my life. Truth has become my reigning thought. I choose to look at the Word of God as a mirror, read it out loud, and make a declaration of who God says I am.

Looking back over the years, I ask myself where I would be if it had not been for God drawing me to Himself and intervening in my thoughts and life. I was on the wide road that was leading me to destruction, but God opened my eyes to see Him, and I made a choice to put my trust in Him. I fell in love with the One and only amazing God-a man named Jesus.

Application

Take a good look at your thought life and the state of your mind. How are your thoughts impacting everyday decisions? Are your thoughts working for you to bring about positive change? Are your thoughts moving you closer to the plan God has for you? Who do your thoughts say you are? How are your thoughts impacting your identity and destiny? What will you do with the next thought that drives you into sadness or deep darkness? Will you stay in self-pity, or will you take authority and drive the negative thoughts into the pit of hell where they belong?

Just like me, you have untapped potential. God has a plan for your life that is yet to be discovered. The closer you come to God, the more you will discover who you are, and why you are here. Begin by praying. Ask God to use all the bad in your life for His good. Ask Him to turn all negativity around to work in your favor. God has never let me down, and I know He will not let you down either. Make yourself available to God and talk to Him about your thoughts, decisions, and life. The Most High God deeply loves and nurtures you.

Questions

1. What is the first thought you had about yourself this morning?

2. What does the Word of God say about who you are?

3. What thoughts and beliefs, do you experience that you need to take captive and submit unto God's Word?

chapter 2
The Heart of a Child

Whosoever therefore shall humble himself as this little child, the same is greatest in the kingdom of heaven.
Matthew 18:4 KJV

I've heard the purest form of who you are shows itself by age six. When I was a young child, my mother always told me I had a heart of gold. Wouldn't it be wonderful if we could all tap into our innermost childlike being—pure and simple?

Unfortunately, over time, life experiences change the person we were born to be into who we become. We become stronger and harder so we can endure and survive. Thankfully, we can get back in touch with our inner purity by delving into the purpose God puts into our hearts.

Everyone has a story and all our stories matter. Looking back at where we came from can help us reunite with the core of who we are. No doubt, we will encounter pain as we look back, as everyone experienced difficult times at one point or another. Deception comes to play when we believe we are the only one who has ever been through anything. We can live in victory today by looking beyond the pain and finding hope in Jesus as He sits with us, talks with us, and walks with us through the storms of life. He knows our stories and everything about us. He's been with us the whole time, guiding us to Himself.

A Pure Heart

As a child, I had a heart of compassion, which often led me to make new friends with kids who were poor. The poor white girls, the poor black girls, and the poor black boys were my friends. I remember feeling accepted when I was with my friends. We would make tents, play house, and tells stories of what we wanted to be when we grew up. I wanted to be a movie star. One of my friends wanted to own a big house and have lots of dinner parties. It was fun to fantasize about the future; it was certainly a great escape from our reality.

One day, a little boy from up the road came to school wearing shoes with holes in them. His clothes were torn and tattered, and he had a dirty, dusty face. Some people called him "the little nappy-headed boy." I befriended him and wanted to help by giving him food, soap, and clothes. At six-years-old, I wrapped up some soap and took it to school for my friend. I remember seeing the commercials on television of the starving children in Africa and wanting to send them something too.

Even among my friends, none of them were close to me. It was rare for me to engage in a deep conversation. Friends did not come to stay the night or weekend. I talked and laughed with my friends at school, but as "cliques" formed, I didn't seem to fit into any of them. I am still that way. The idea of being a part of any particular group does not appeal to me. I have always made choices without looking to others to influence me. My mother was the only person I looked to for guidance.

At school, there was a group of "popular" black girls who found pleasure in being the school bullies. They were mean, picked on me, called me names, and laughed at me. I remember their jeers and how they would single me out. From kindergarten to third grade, because of the way the mean kids treated me, most of my friends continued to be other marginalized misfits like me.

After years of bullying, being laughed at, and picked on, I became defensively angry and reacted to every little thing. I wore my feelings on my sleeve. By the time I made it to junior high, I was tired of being the target and started standing up for myself. I was fighting every week. The anger in me was real.

I would be fussing in an argument with a girl or a boy, then all of a sudden, I would become extremely outraged and jump on them, taking out all of my frustration and anger. In junior high, my nickname was Muhammad Ali: "Float like a butterfly; stung like a bee." Once I gained ground and established I was not putting up with the ridicule any longer, the bullies left me alone. I now had a new problem; I was alone with my anger.

As a young person, I did not realize I should be trying to figure out what was causing the pain inside of me. I felt as if I was watching life move around me, while the real me stayed trapped inside. Unconsciously, I began searching for significance. I began to seek solutions in people. I didn't realize other people were just like me, never able to fulfill their needs.

My Diary

I remember the day Mother handed me a little blue book that had its own little lock and key. A diary! Mother told me writing in my diary would help me to understand all the feelings inside of me. No one knew the truth of what I had been through, or what I was experiencing. I didn't even understand where the fits of rage, triggered by the smallest agitations, came from. My mind was bound to shame and guilt. I had no idea how to express what was going on with me.

That little diary was the only place I felt safe to express myself. My diary held the secrets of my heart. I wrote about the hurt, pain, and shame inside of me. I took my diary wherever I went. One day, I hid my diary in the attic so no one would ever find it. Then the unthinkable happened. One of my sisters found my diary in the attic and began to read it aloud. I was so embarrassed. I began to retreat into the shell of safety I had created for myself and added another layer of shame. Shame, shame, and more shame.

My method of coping was to internalize everything. Every external issue went inward until it created an emotional jungle. My young impressionable spirit did not know how to handle my life except to let it build up inside of me. Eventually, I began to overflow, and my inner pain came out in negative ways. I did not know it then, but I now know my behavior was a scream for help.

When I look back over my life and see where I was and where I am today, I am so grateful to be alive. It is only by the grace of God I'm not dead. There were many issues and circumstances that could have destroyed me. The first incident happened when, as a toddler, I curiously wanted to find out what was in my dad's cup. It was hot coffee. The cup turned over, spewed the liquid onto my chest, and severely burned my torso. I still have scars. I thank God the coffee did not splatter onto my face.

Later, the pain of my teenage years was unbearable, even too much for me to express in this book. By the grace of God, I made it out of my teenage years alive. I have made mistakes and moral failure after moral failure. Plainly, I am a flawed, broken, mess. But I thank God, He looked beyond my state and saw the underlying pain I was experiencing. God's strength proved to be enough for me, especially in my weaknesses.

I Have Overcome

With everything I have been through, I have learned the power words have over the outcome of every situation.

Speaking words of life keeps me pushing toward my goals. As a young person, I would look in the mirror and tell myself, "I am somebody. I am going to make something out of my life." Verbal affirmations kept me going in school, empowered me to work hard, and eventually led me to pursue higher education.

There is power in the spoken word. There is power in believing in yourself. Living a life of self-defeat is impossible when there is hope. Jesus said we could move mountains, even if our faith is only the size of a mustard seed. Even in the bad times of life, I have held onto mustard seed faith. Holding on, even to a small amount of faith, has done so much in my life.

Mother planted words of affirmation, and seeds of faith and hope into me. There were times when my mom would tell me, "Teresa, I like the way you wash the dishes. You do such a good job." Those words alone made me want to go into the kitchen and wash dishes. My mom never put me down. Maybe she could sense my fragile nature or low self-esteem. She knew it was important to treat her children with care and compassion.

There is power in our speech. Words can lift, or they can tear down. Negative words or verbal abuse can emotionally kill someone. Hearing constant criticism causes us not to be able to trust enough to open up and express what is going on internally. The bullying I experienced, along with other abuses throughout my teenage years, broke my confidence in people. The guilty, shameful, and dirty feelings I had kept me trapped. As a child, I carried a heavy weight, burdened with shame by no fault of my own. God only knows the thoughts that went through my mind.

It is a miracle that in His love, God intervened. As a child, my Heavenly Father began to teach me to believe in myself and to know I was somebody to Him. He gave me joy and hope to look in the mirror and say to myself, "God cares about me. I am somebody." How did I make it through the early years without being thoroughly ruined for life? It was the words of life from God, my mother, and myself that kept me, and helped me to push through all the bad.

Lessons Learned

Along with learning to speak words of affirmation over my life, I learned I could not hide anything from God. God knows everything about me and loves me even when all my issues are out in the open. The lies I told by putting up a front, and the secrets I tried to hide all came out in the open as I stood before God.

God kept His hand on my life through every situation. His love for me has never changed, even during the most difficult years. As I recount the limitless times God spoke up for me, went before me, and changed entire environments for me, I have no doubt I will be alright no matter what the future holds. God has never let me down. He has never failed me. He is my best friend.

I've learned to peel back the layers, and to take off the masks of defensiveness. As God revealed Himself to me, I must transparently reveal myself to Him. Standing before God honestly, open, and broken, He reveals what He put in me from the very beginning—a heart of gold. With God's help, I've torn down the walls I built around myself and learned to live life with a heart full of compassion and care for the people around me.

In the same way, let your light shine before others, that they may see your good deeds and glorify your Father in heaven.
Matthew 5:16 NIV

Application

You cannot move forward if you are still dealing with the pain from your past. It's time to heal and live your life to the fullest, trusting God every step of the way. The journey to freedom will not be a walk in the park. There will be many challenges along the way. God promises He will be with us as we walk through life. Regardless if the valley is long and winding or quick and short, God walks with us through it. Knowing God is always here keeps us from experiencing the paralyzing feelings of fear. He wants to give us the complete healing we need. He wants us to have His thoughts and walk in His ways.

When God created human beings in His image, He wanted us to walk in intimate harmony with Him. God had a beautiful plan for mankind, but He gave us a choice. He allows us to hide if we want to, as Adam and Eve did. He calls for us to come out of hiding, and to show the pure core of who we are—our innocent inner child. It's easy for us to be distracted and fade away from God's ways. The enemy of our souls knows the precise circumstances and temptations to entice us away. Let's humble ourselves before God, realize our susceptibility, peel back the layers we've hidden ourselves in, and allow God to recreate us in His image.

Questions

1. What are you hiding from yourself and God? Is it possibly pain, shame, or guilt? Maybe grief, disappointment, or heartache?

2. Have you protected yourself inside of layers of defense? Do pride, fear, or mistrust have you trapped inside? What are the layers protecting you made of?

3. Think back to when you were a young child. What were your strengths? What was your pure heart like?

4. Write out an affirmation based on the characteristics of your pure, child-like heart. Place the affirmation somewhere you can see it, and read it aloud every day. Stand before God unafraid, and allow Him to reveal your heart of gold.

chapter 3
An Identity Free of Shame

Those who look to him are radiant;
their faces are never covered with shame.
Psalm 34:5 NIV

Our minds hold onto everything. We never know when an old thought or feeling will emerge. Sometimes, even when I am at my highest moments, a memory from forty years ago comes of out of nowhere, and shame hits me like a ton of bricks. The feeling weighs heavily on my emotional vein, causing a sudden wave of depression. The heaviness of shame can turn a day of joy into one of sorrow. I had to learn to not to give my negative memories attention, or they would threaten to steal my peace and derail me from God's promise and purpose for my life.

Research defines shame as an emotion which causes a person to feel bad about themselves based on their perceived notion of having sinned or having done something against a moral standard. Shame-based thinking can internalize deep within us, causing anger, resentment, low self-esteem, and other destructive thoughts, which can lead to harmful behaviors.

Not all shame results in negativity. Healthy shame comes from recognizing we have disobeyed God and results in us changing our behavior to align with God's Word. On the other hand, toxic shame causes us to begin to self-identify according to our shame. Instead of recognizing our behavior and modifying it externally, if we internalize toxic shame we begin to feel like a mistake, instead of feeling like a loved person who made a mistake. Some say the internalization of toxic shame develops from a lack of validation, affection, and nurturing as a child.

To being unraveling shame from our identity, we must go back to the time when shame began. It can be a painful journey to reminisce on, but when we recognize our circumstances, we can better define the source of our shame, and discern if it is healthy or toxic. As I share my story, I hope you begin to think about your story, and how it may impact feelings of shame you currently experience.

School Days

When I first started school, I had many teachers who were loving and kind. I remember one teacher who had long, black, shiny hair. She was tall, and she was kind. She was always happy and warm. The coach I had when I was in the first grade always talked to me and made me laugh. I know how the teachers made me feel in kindergarten through second grade, but I do not remember their names or faces. I remember I felt safe, and knew I was important, and belonged. School was a place I trusted.

Chapter 3 · An Identity Free of Shame | 31

My feelings of shame started developing at school. When I was in the first grade, I remember thinking I did not measure up academically with the other students. One of my teachers kept a poster with all the students' names. We could earn gold stars by our names throughout the week. I do not recall the purpose of the chart, or how we earned stars, but I do remember the feeling I had when I realized I was not earning as many stars as my classmates. I felt dumb and stupid. I began to internalize shame.

I started coming to school with a heavy heart. I had low self-esteem, walked with my head hung low, thrived on attention from boys, and had emotional outbursts where I would cry for seemingly no reason. Looking back, it seems my experience from third grade through eighth grade was a season of fighting to survive and to hold onto the last bit of self-esteem left in me.

The "C" Class

After the desegregation of schools in Georgia, a trend emerged to categorize students based on academic ability. I was placed in the "C" classroom. I remember peeking inside of the "A" classroom wondering what went on in that class. Why was I excluded? Were the "A" children better than me?

I viewed myself from a negative perspective because some of the individuals in the "A" and "B" classes flaunted the idea that they were in the smarter classrooms, and that the "C" and "D" classroom kids were slow. Even though none of what they said was true, it influenced how I viewed myself.

So, there I was in the "slow" class with students who couldn't read or were constantly disrupting the classroom by talking, playing, or beating on the desks. I often wondered how the teachers determine I belonged in the "C" class. I never felt challenged academically there.

As I grew older, cliques began to form and the social aspects of being in school became a major focus of my education experience. Unfortunately, ridicule based on academic achievement did not stop. I remember one boy who snickered after making me feel stupid in front of the whole fifth-grade class. He was the school nerd, a smart guy, and his arrogance was second to none. I was a below-average type of student according to the system that placed me in the "C" class.

Despite feeling dumb, I was not dumb. Though I did not remember most of the things I learned in school, I had no problem taking tests and making good grades. I never took books home to study, and always completed my homework before leaving school for the day or, at the latest, I'd finish it on the bus. The work was too easy for me. I wanted to learn something I could actually apply to my life.

I had an "aha" moment in my fifth-grade social studies class. We were learning about setting short-term and long-term goals. Finally, a concept I could apply to my life! I began setting goals for my studies and other areas of my life. I can't remember anything else I learned in school that year, but the process of setting goals is still with me today.

I Have Overcome

In my professional opinion as a teacher, categorizing kids into classes based on academic performance does not have a positive impact on any students' achievement. Research studies have shown that ability grouping may, in fact, have a negative effect on student perceptions and student academic achievement. Academically average students placed with high-performing students end up performing at higher levels. On the other hand, students placed in low-ability groups do not show significant gains in achievement (Gomora, Nystrand, Berends, LePore, 1995).

Keeping students separated keeps those who think they are not as bright as the others in a place of inferiority. Instead of building them up, and teaching them through the example of other students, children like myself were kept isolated without the chance to improve.

I thank God I had an unquenchable desire for knowledge and understanding. As a young child, I would read the dictionary and encyclopedias for enjoyment. I was destined to become a scholar. I am so glad God knew my heart's desire. I wanted more knowledge, and I sought it out. I began spending the majority of my time in the library. After graduating high school, I went to college.

Now, at the age of forty-seven, I have earned my doctoral degree, the highest of educational pursuits. I thank God for helping me to overcome feelings of shame and inadequacy that began in childhood, and that could have kept me from moving forward in life. My next goal is to write, research, and create masterpieces. I want to fully tap into my creativity and unlock my ultimate God-given potential. I don't have all the answers as to why some things happened in my life, but I know what I've survived and how it has helped make me who I am today.

Lessons Learned

As an adult, I realize the younger me adopted my teacher's gold-star reward system, my "C" status, and the taunts of bullies. As a result, I experienced a negative self-image. Those strong feelings left a mark, as I still have the memories today as a middle-aged woman.

There were times as an adult I could have easily internalized shame, and based my identity and self-perception on what others said about me. For example, some people can recount my sins better than I can. Those are the people who have nothing better to do than to sit around and fester over the failures of others, instead of spending time on their own personal growth and development. Their words and assumptions could damage me if I allowed them to.

The key to handling petty people such as these, is to view them as a sad case and to pray for them, but to keep them at arm's length. It will do no good to hate the people that hate me; hate is not constructive. I choose to hold onto Dr. Martin Luther King, Jr.'s philosophy of showing love: "Love drives out hate, and light drives the darkness away."

The negative opinions of others do not matter. Do not give anyone on this earth the power to control or limit you from the life God has for you. God is the one with the power, and when we pursue the dreams He puts inside of us, nothing can hold us back. Moving into the supernatural realm of thought will take concentration and focus, but it's not impossible. No matter what anyone says, pursue your passion! As I venture out into God's plans and dreams for my life, sometimes I still feel uncertain, but I continue to move forward.

Application

It's easy for us to internalize the shame other people impose on us. Even as adults, many of us are bound to people pleasing—trying to gain approval through good works, thus avoiding shame. Sometimes, we even try to perform to please God and gain His love and acceptance. It is easy to fear what other people think or say of us, and end up falling into the performance trap. It's especially easy to feel shame when we are around people who are negative and put us down. Again, remember that some say internalizing toxic shame is a result of a lack of validation, affection, and nurturing. If shame can overwhelm a child, it can also overwhelm an adult.

To overcome shame, I learned to lean into God's love. God's love and acceptance cannot be earned from being good enough or doing enough good deeds. His love is already settled in Heaven. Jesus died for my sins, and no bad deed or lack of good deeds can take away His love.

What if everyone lived to their fullest intelligence without allowing their mind, other people, reward systems, or bullies to hold them back? What if we knew how much God loves us, and the good things He wants to do in and through our lives? It's time to release the inhibitions that keep us from fully expressing all the gifts God has put within us.

Questions

1. Are there any people in your life that set you up to fall into the shame trap?

2. What are you doing to guard your thoughts and mind against toxic shame?

3. Are there any areas in your life where you are experiencing healthy shame and need to submit your behaviors to the Word of God?

chapter 4
A Prosperous Life

For I know the plans I have for you," declares the Lord,
"plans to prosper you and not to harm you,
plans to give you hope and a future.
Jeremiah 29:11 NIV

Poverty's whisper lingers even after gaining financial prosperity. A person raised in poverty can become the most educated in the universe, but until there is shift in their belief system, their pockets will still be bare, with no visible financial progress. A process of changing old thoughts and habits is required to reverse the devastating impact of growing up in an impoverished family. People bound to a mindset of poverty are stuck in the "just making it" line of thinking, and never go beyond to prosperity, even when they are no longer poor A mindset of poverty enslaves a person to circumstances, and offers no hope for change.

In my experience, even after I had money, I continued to purchase consumer products that quickly depreciated. I bought cheap items because I didn't see the value of the more expensive brands. I ended up spending more in the long run. I came from a large family where we didn't spend money on unnecessary name brands, or high-quality anything. When the "poor man" mentality is all a person has ever known, it's hard to break away from old habits.

To transition from impoverished to prosperity, we must change our values. Our mindsets must shift to a "wealthy" view point. Our identity must embody prosperous beliefs, such as: "I am rich, not poor. I have all I need and more. My life is full of abundance. I am accumulating wealth. God is supplying all my needs according to His riches and glory." Having a prosperous mindset is not about how much money you have, but about approaching and experiencing life from a place of gratefulness instead of lack.

Growing Up Poor

I wish I could have severed myself from poverty at the root of my beginnings, but somehow poverty bound my family together. We developed a commonality of need and want. We wanted laughter. We wanted to "feel good," even if it only lasted a week. When there was an abundance of food, we would all act giggly and silly, dancing around the house. We would joke and have a good time as we enjoyed food during times of joy. Then, as the days went by, the refrigerator would become barer and barer. The cycle of poverty would continue. Times of abundance led to times of want, all in a matter of a week or two. As the food went away, so did our laughter.

I remember the struggle. Wintertime was the most difficult. At times, there was no heat in the house and no food on the table. I remember ice-cold floors and clothes piled up on the bed to keep us warm. Gas was our only source of heat. When the gas tanks were empty, the house was frigid. There was a heater in the hallway, and one in the living room, which helped to take the chill off the house.

It's a wonder that our home never caught fire with eight little children running around those heaters. As a child, the house seemed spacious, but as an adult, I revisited the two-bedroom house, and it was very small inside. All my siblings and I slept nestled in a tiny room with one full-sized bed, one twin bed, and a bunkbed set. We all had to share; I guess that's why we are so close-knit.

The times when the gas tank ran out resulted in having no heat. You see, our house in the woods was heated by old fashioned gas heaters. The struggle was real, the cold was real, and the mornings waking up to an ice-cold floor was real. The pot of boiling hot water that we poured into a foot tub to bathe in was real. We did not have indoor plumbing for a long time, so I will leave it up to your imagination on how we used the restroom in those early days living out in the country in McGregor, Georgia.

My narrative is not isolated from others who lived on that long dirt road. Many others had similar struggles sustaining through the cold winter months. I thank God for the journey because it taught me the value of appreciating both the good times and the bad times. Through it all, we had the main ingredient, and that was love for each other.

Despite our struggles, my mom did her best to make sure we had what we needed. She worked the three to eleven shifts at the nursing home in the city of Vidalia. I remember days where we would get off the school bus starving, and come home to find Mom had prepared a fully cooked meal before she left for work, and it was waiting for us on the stove. The fried chicken, sweet peas, mashed potatoes, sweet potatoes, corn bread, and Kool-Aid were delectable after a long day at school.

A Spirit of Poverty

It wasn't just a lack of money that ruled our house; it was a striving-for-more, which sometimes included violence. We played cards with our daddy for dimes, nickels, and quarters. If we had the good fortune of winning, Daddy would demand we give all the money back to him. He had a drinking problem, which is where those extra dimes and nickels went.

When Daddy was in a drunken stupor, we would go through his pockets to find loose change. The next day, the fury would begin. His cursing, hell-raising, and violence would terrorize our little house in the woods. My mom would plead with whoever took Daddy's change to please give it back to spare the family.

As children, we spent many days waiting outside in the dark until our mother came home from work at eleven o'clock at night. We would look over the small hill on the road to see the headlights and would sing our song, "HERE COMES JOHNNIE, JOHNNIE, JOHNNIE!" Our mom was our hero. She was the one who made everything alright with her love, despite the poverty around us.

I Have Overcome

The cycle of moving from poverty to abundance, and back to poverty followed me into adulthood. I have had times of plenty and times of barely anything. God is still in the process of healing the impoverished areas of my life. He is changing the thoughts and subconscious belief system I learned as a child who grew up in a small two-bedroom house with seven siblings and two parents. Poverty is a disease I've battled, self-medicating along the way with "Band-Aid" solutions when I needed intensive care around the clock.

The effects of my childhood poverty mentality spilled over into my adult life and impacted every financial decision I made. Striving to fill an emotional void, I would buy cars, clothes, jewelry, and other items, which led to a black hole in my finances. Even the pursuit of higher education, which should ensure I would not be stuck in poverty, came with a very costly price tag. The cost of education, undoubtedly, was one the most expensive decisions I made in my life.

For a long time, I experienced a constant striving for more. I was striving to not be poor. In the process, at times my bank account balance would be zero, or in the negative. When that happened, depressive feelings and horrid memories of "not having" overwhelmed me, telling me emptiness is how it would always be. "You will always struggle financially," was my self-defeating narrative, and it was a lie. I believed the lies for so long; I became a prisoner of my self-limiting beliefs about money.

My thoughts had to change for me to start altering the reality of my financial state. I was living with a poverty mindset, even though I had an education, a good paying job, and a husband with a good paying job. I began to develop a mindset of wealth, to shift my thoughts from lack to abundance. Poverty is a generational curse that I have to fight in the battlefield of my mind.

I walk in faith daily believing that God always makes a way out of no way. He will open and shut financial doors no human has power over. The journey to changing my belief system about money has not been easy, but centering my thoughts on God's provision has changed every aspect of my life.

Life can strip away a great deal from us, but one thing it cannot take is the love of God from our hearts. God's provision has sustained me day after day, even in times of loss and poverty. The devil tried his best to kill me, to destroy me, and to drain my sense of self-worth, but the streets did not take my life. Somehow, God restored my joy and kept me from the worst of what could have happened. Instead of taking my life, poverty taught me to persevere through difficult, tough, and bitter times.

I no longer strive for wealth. I surrender my needs and desires to my Creator. I trust He will provide what I need, and what He wants me to have. My identity is no longer bound to the materialistic things of life. My emotional state is not dependent on how much money I have in my bank account to indulge in. With God's help, I push through thoughts of self-preservation and move into a place of abundance where, by faith, I sow financially into God's kingdom and reap God's provision.

Lessons Learned

When I think about the amount of money that has passed through my hands over the years, I know I would have been wealthy by now if I handled it differently. I would avoid the debt trap if I were given a chance to reverse the damage it has caused to my financial peace. Consumer debt and student loan debt are two of the most incapacitating obstacles I currently face.

I viewed student loan debt as an investment, but I have yet to see a dynamic return on my huge investment. Colleges sell higher education with a promise of future careers that pay three times as much as we spend on education, but once we graduate no one is standing there waiting to offer us an amazing job. Regardless of securing a well-paying job or not, we are still responsible for paying our student loans.

My consumer debt is less easy to justify. I admit I've had a lot of greed and bought things I wanted that I really couldn't afford. Cars, clothes, and other materialistic items misled me into thinking I would be happy if I had more. The truth is, no object can ever bring inner joy, peace, or fulfillment. Only a relationship with Jesus can supply our heart's needs. In Luke 12:29-31 (NLT), the Bible says, "And don't be concerned about what to eat and what to drink. Don't worry about such things. These things dominate the thoughts of unbelievers all over the world, but your Father already knows your needs. Seek the Kingdom of God above all else, and he will give you everything you need."

When we follow God's divine order, keeping God first and allow everything else to follow, God will provide. He provided for the children of Israel in the wilderness with manna (bread) from heaven. In His Word, God repeatedly tells us to seek Him first, and everything else will follow. He is our Provider. Success, prosperity, and abundance only come through Him. Some of the Israelites did not trust God's promises, followed the road of doubt, and chose to do life their way. God's way is the best way because He sees and knows all things, and He will give us just what we need. I've learned trusting God yields huge dividends. Jesus is the way, the truth, and the life (John 4:16).

I learned a lot from growing up in a loving home that was caught in a cycle of poverty. I learned to be grateful for everything God has given me. I learned to work hard, to be diligent and self-sufficient in this life. My past does not predicate who I am becoming. The past taught me many lessons, but I moved on to a higher thought life. God elevated my thoughts to the point where I am no longer poor, but rich in every area.

Though I have grown and changed, growing up in poverty planted seeds of fear in me. I am still afraid that one day I will be impoverished. I fear losing all I've gained. I fear not measuring up, or that somehow, I am living a lie. I must pull up the weeds of doubt poverty planted, which give me a sense I am undeserving and unworthy of a life of abundance. Shifting my thoughts begins with acknowledging all my thoughts and feelings, and confronting the destructive parts. I am committed to changing my mindset, empowered by the truth: "I am worthy to have a happy, blessed, and prosperous life. My Father is rich, and He loves me."

Application

There is no one formula for overcoming poverty. We each must begin a meta-cognitive analysis of our thoughts on the role money plays in life. Consider the big picture of the amount of money that goes through your hands throughout your entire life. We each have the opportunity to grow what we have, or to waste it.

People who live in a financially broken state, unsure of where the next dollar will come from, experience a strange form of anxiety that haunts them from the time they wake up until the time they go to sleep. The feelings do not go away. The pressure drives them away from rest and into a place of fear and strife. Every bit of energy goes to push them to pursue money instead of pursing God.

Research studies show that poverty impacts children's brains because they are exposed to high levels of stress early on. Poverty also impacts academic performance and behavior. Poverty is a road many travel, and sadly some end up in a bottomless pit with no hope for the future. Despite its risks and challenges, poverty can teach us many good lessons and develop stronger character within us. It is possible for those who have lived a life of poverty to gain a sense of helplessness in the face of trial after trial, deprivation, and neediness. We can choose to end up in a pit or choose to allow trials to purify us.

The choices we make related to money, relationships, and health reveals much about areas of weaknesses. Poor financial choices uncover underlying issues we need to deal with that may not even be related to money. The way I have handled my financial life reflects the other areas of my life.

Like me, maybe you have tried to fill an emotional void through spending. Perhaps, you find self-worth in what you own. Or maybe you lack understanding on how money works. There is no one solution to the money issue because all our problems are different. Becoming aware of the root of our financial woes is the beginning of a journey of freedom.

Our relationship with money is both emotional and spiritual. Our childhood experiences, education, and exposure to higher levels of thinking shapes the views we have about money. We can either allow our views to remain as is, or we can self-educate and begin to change the paradigm of the beliefs that have negatively impacted us. We are our own change agents.

Questions

1. Begin an assessment of your thought life and search out if anything is keeping you bound financially. What is your core belief about money? How did that core belief develop?

2. What are your financial priorities? What place does faith in God have in your finances?

3. Look back over the past five years of your tax returns. How much money has passed through your hands during that time? How much money did you invest? How much did you waste?

4. What do you want to see come out of the next five years of the money that you have power over?

5. Do you have a clear understanding of financial principals? Is there any area you need to gain knowledge about to help yourself move out of poverty and forward into prosperity?

chapter 5
Rebuilding Trust

When I am afraid, I put my trust in You.
Psalm 56:3 NIV

Relationships are built on a base of trust over time, and can tear a part in the moment trust is broken. How many of us can say we have quality relationships filled with trust in this world where everyone looks out for themselves? Too often, families don't look out for one another. Rather, they sit in judgment and discuss each other's shortcomings and downfalls. What good can come from gossiping, slandering, or casting a negative shadow on the life of the people we say we love and care about?

Those of us who have lived around unsupportive and unproductive people know how effortlessly they can drain our passion for life and the things that once brought us pleasure and joy. When we are dealing with relationships that lack trust, it is easy to drift further away from God's grace and sink into the smothering grave of the death of dreams. Dreams won't survive in an environment of negativity.

Once trust is compromised, forgiveness and reconciliation are required to repair a broken relationship. Restoration can be tumultuous at times, but all things are possible through God. Rebuilding trust seems to be left to the mature, the confident, and those who don't judge others based on failures. We must rise above listening to scorn and verbal abuse, and save each other from drowning in the sea of despair.

Letting Go and Letting God

It is difficult to trust after being. Walls that create boundaries are formed after bad experiences. Getting through the pain takes much prayer and time. Broken trust happens when lies are told. We all long to experience God's repairing power after being a painful experience. How does one rebuild broken trust? As said before, it takes prayer. It takes God. It takes all parties involved being willing to start over. It takes the power of forgiveness. God is able.

Failed Attempts at Love

When we look for love in the wrong places, we are bound to find the wrong kind of love. Many of us fall into the belief that people can fill our love tanks. We believe we are truly I in love, when, in fact, both parties are empty, each trying to meet their needs through the other. If they only knew that real love comes from a relationship with God. Empty vessels cannot fill empty vessels. Instead of coming into a relationship with a healthy perception of love, both parties enter the relationship lost, torn, broken not possessing what it takes to fulfill the other's needs.

Growing in the Love of God

My deepest feeling of love came when I surrendered to Jesus. The flood of love I felt in that moment of my history washed away all dirty and shameful feelings that weighed so heavily on my shoulders.

The key to victory is a genuine, trusting relationship with God. My relationship with God is the foundation that keeps my life intact. No doubt, without Him I could do nothing, but nothing is impossible with Him. He interrupts my thoughts with His thoughts of care and love.

God gives me plenty of room to make independent decisions, but in the end, He is there helping and guiding me to the place He wants me to be. I pray God leads me into authentic relationships that draw me closer to Him. I want the type of relationship that inspires me to serve the Lord in greater ways. I want relationships in which I inspire others to greatness.

Lessons Learned

After God transformed my self-worth with His love, He began teaching me healthy boundaries. Setting boundaries is healthy. Healthy boundaries are for me and the people who I love. I have the power to teach others how I wish to be treated. If I allow myself to receive love, I will get it. If I allow myself to be used, I will get used. I don't have to respond to my critics. I know who I am in Christ. I must admit, sometimes I take boundaries too far, and I cannot block people out. I often have held fast to my invisible walls in a desperate attempt to try to protect myself. God is still working on me in this area of my life. I am trusting God through this process of learning to forget about the past and pressing forward. I am walking in the truth that I must let go and let God have His way.

Application

I once heard someone describe "fear" as an acronym. F.E.A.R. stands for "False Evidence Appearing Real." Some experts propose the way to deal with our fear is to embrace it. The idea is to be willing to be in a state of discomfort to accomplish goals.

To move forward, we must deal with the fear standing in our way. If you struggle to build trusting relationships, you likely are experiencing much fear: fear of failure, fear of success, fear of rejection, and fear of what people will think. The list of what we fear goes on to infinity, each false piece of evidence presenting itself as real.

Sometimes, our minds tend to create fantastic and unreal stories. How many of us have imagined scenarios where people cross our boundaries and break our trust? Those dramatic escapades are based on fear, which causes us to envision negative possibilities.

The Word of God says we are to "cast down imaginations and every high thing that exalts itself against the knowledge of God, bringing into captivity every thought to the obedience of Christ" (2 Corinthians 10:5). Living in fear keeps us from obeying the will of God. Nothing great has ever been accomplished without taking risks and stepping out on faith, including building trusting relationships.

Questions

1. Do you struggle to trust people? What about trusting God?

2. What happened in your past to break your trust? Can you pinpoint the broken relationship at the root of your struggle?

3. Do you depend on anyone or anything other than God to fill the void broken relationships have left in your heart?

4. What are you doing to learn to trust again?

5. Do you have healthy boundaries that help you to distinguish who is trustworthy and who is not?

chapter 6
From Insecurity to Success

I can do all things through Christ which strengtheneth me.
Philippians 4:13 KJV

There comes a time when we must spread our wings, despite any insecurity we may feel. We cannot depend on what we learned in college. We must trust God and rely on what He planted in us long before our formal education.

The accomplishments in my life come from God. He led me to the place I am today. If it had not been for the Lord, I don't know where I would be. As I write about my accomplishments, I think about the road I traveled to arrive where I am today. It was a road of trials, tribulations, and fear, some of which I brought upon myself.

As I write this chapter on insecurity, I write with many insecurities still plaguing me. In the back of my mind, I always think, "What will people think if I write *this* in my book?" I long to be authentic in every way, even concerning my insecurities.

Struggles are real, and I still have my share of them, but not as many as I had before I surrendered it all to Jesus. Failures do not have to keep me from accomplishing my dreams in life. In fact, failures are stepping stones that can lead me higher and propel me into my destiny. I thank God for wisdom He placed in me to discern the difference between right and wrong. He has delivered me from the snares of the enemy that kept me bound for so long.

God Planted Success into My Heart

The success I now experience began as a seed God planted in my heart as a child. I have previously written about some of the dysfunction I grew up in and had to overcome. Emotional memories still invade my mind and are sometimes tough to shake away. Thankfully, I had some positive formative experiences that gave me hope. I built on my small successes and learned to move forward to create the life I desired.

At the age of four, or five, I remember going on an errand for my mother to the store to buy bread, peanut butter, and jelly. I bought what my mom asked for and went straight back home. I was too young to be walking to the store by myself, but she must have known I was mature and smart enough to handle it. That trip to the store left me feeling light and free, filled with an indescribable, overwhelming joy and confidence.

As a child, I enjoyed reading and researching about two very different subjects: black history and algebraic concepts. One of my favorite pastimes was reading my mother's set of encyclopedias. At the age of six or seven, though I wasn't the best reader, I would look at the pages depicting the Civil

Rights Movement. I was moved with compassion when I saw Rosa Parks on the bus, and as I looked through pictures of black people being sprayed with water hoses. The images were forever painted in my memory and supplied me with fuel to do something positive with my life. God began establishing social consciousness within me. My siblings and I would talk about social injustice, and what we should do about it.

Learning about the oppression other people faced was not the only factor that motivated me to push through my insecurities. Working in the deep south cropping hot tobacco fields was miserable. I told myself I was not going to spend my life in a hot field. "I am going to be *somebody* one day," I would say to myself. I believed in myself beyond the limited ideas other people had about me.

My curiosity and love of learning became one of my greatest strengths to propel me forward and out of insecurity. In college, I became confident in myself as a scholar, and have stayed in "school mode" for most my adult life. I enjoy the structure, intellectual challenges, and deadlines. School was something I could work toward, and succeed at.

After graduating high school, I started attending a technical college in Swainsboro, Georgia. I earned several certificates in secretarial-related skills. After that, my family suffered a crisis, and I had to put my educational pursuits on hold. I never returned to the technical college in Swainsboro. Instead, I applied and was accepted at Brewton Parker College.

I attended two semesters at BPC, and another tragedy struck my family. I had to withdraw from school completely and did not return for many years. Before I went back to BPC, I enrolled at Southeastern Technical College and graduated with an Information Office Technology degree. After that, I enrolled again at Brewton Parker College and completed two associate's degrees and one bachelor's degree.

I continued my educational pursuits by enrolling at Georgia Southern University, where I graduated with a Master's in Education and an Educational Specialist degree. My most recent academic achievement is finishing my doctoral degree.

Some people questioned why I pursued so much education. I asked myself that question as well. Research contends social cues causes one to pursue activities they associate with success. I realized the accomplishments I have obtained came with the reward of recognition. My initial success in education led me to pursue further degree-related successes.

I Have Overcome

Looking back over my life, and examining my strengths and weaknesses allows me to identify areas of my life where I need to improve and focus my attention. Nothing is impossible when we set our mind on a goal, trust God with all our heart, and take intentional action.

At times, setting goals seemed pointless and vain, especially when I consider the brevity of life. Lately, my thoughts have centered on looking back at the goals I have accomplished as I ponder what should be next in my goal-setting and success journey.

I am no longer in pursuit of success related to education. The place I am today moves me to set goals unrelated to earning a college degree. Reaching higher and higher, and digging deeper and deeper within myself to come to this place of self-discovery took much time and thought. Now, it is time to use my degrees and skills to add significant value to the world around me by giving myself to the greater good of my community and church.

I have set my sights on becoming financially free and physically fit. I am striving for a healthy and growing marriage, where we set goals together to be as successful as we can be. My goal is to successfully raise my son to be a fine young man who makes a difference in the world. He already has a strong character and a heart for other people. I am so proud of him.

Application

Today is the day to make wise decisions, to set SMART goals and to move forward. Past events do not define who we are, or what we can accomplish. We only have TODAY. Many do not achieve their goals because they allow something in their past to hold them back. Freedom is what Christ came to give us. Freedom from fear. Freedom from thinking negatively about oneself. Freedom from rejection.

Freedom from limitations. Freedom from oppression and those who oppress.

Maybe you have struggled with setting goals and accomplishing the desires of your heart. Take some time to write down the three most important goals you have personally, professionally, and financially. Begin to write out some action steps of what it will take for you to reach your goals. Invest in a cork board and index cards to write your goals on, and pin the written goals somewhere visible. Keep your goals in front of you as a visual reminder.

Share your goals with your spouse or a trusted friend. Have them pray with you, and keep you accountable to sticking to your goals. You will not attain your goals overnight. You must work toward your goal daily to see small changes. Don't give up. The small changes will add up. Keep your focus on the result, and you too will reach your goals.

Questions

1. Look back over your life and childhood. What successes did God plant in your heart as a child and young person? How have those successes shaped your adult goals and accomplishments?

2. Do you have any limiting thought or belief about yourself that you need to update to achieve your goals?

3. What is your goal for this week? This month? This year? The next five years? Ten years? If you don't have long-term goals, it's okay. Start with what you have, and ask God to give you His vision for your life.

chapter 7
Chains are Broken

I will go before you and will level the mountains; I will break down gates of bronze and cut through bars of iron.
Isaiah 42:2

The pain of abuse stole away the childhood that was so rightfully mine. It awakened feelings that a five or six-year-old should never have. If it had not been for the Lord where would I be? I am free. Praise the Lord! I am free! The pain took many years of joy from my life, but I am here now and my joy overflows.

At the age of 21, I went back and confronted the abuser that committed the heinous evil act against me. I faced the darkness. I confronted the shame that tried to keep me in darkness, making me feel as if I did something wrong. I did nothing wrong. The devil is a liar. If he can keep sin hidden in the dark and cover us with shame, freedom will never come. We must expose the shame, expose the darkness, and bring it into the light so God can heal the pain.

God healed me 28 years ago. I pray my story will set someone else free from their shame, and horrid past. God loves you. He wants to wash away your pain, shame, and defeat. He wants to turn your mourning into dancing and give you beauty for the ash heaps in your life. Don't let the devil win. Come out of the hidden places, let go, and let God apply the healing Balm of Gilead.

Through abuse, the devil planted an unclean spirit inside of my mind and body. The unclean spirit's purpose was to kill me, to rob me of all self-esteem and joy, to ultimately drain all life from me. My mind became enslaved to the darkness of sad memories at a very early age, and I tried to bury the pain deep within my subconscious mind. Depression, loneliness, bitterness, anger, and low self-image led me deeper into darkness, but it didn't kill me. I am alive and an overcomer writing my story.

The Lord saved me in 1989. After God rescued me, He took me through a process of healing. It was a step-by-step journey. He brought the right people into my life at the right time and supplied my every need.

After the Lord saved me, it still took some time for me to grow and heal from all of the hurt in my life. It seemed there was something about me that attracted unhealthy relationships. In reality, there was not anything wrong with me, except for the lies the devil planted in my head. I had many feelings of unworthiness, which tried to hold me captive.

The beginning of my pain came from the summer days, evenings, and nights as I was molested in the backwoods of McGregor, Georgia. I will never forget the smell of that barn and the confusion I had, or feeling of liquid running down my legs. I didn't know what was going on. I was a six-year-old little girl.

Years later, I went to my abuser and his mother, my great aunt, to let them both know that I remembered what happened to me and that I forgive them. There was no acknowledgment of the rapes and no repentance. Maybe it was all too taboo for them to acknowledge, a hidden history they never wanted to be spoken aloud. But it was true, and I confronted the offender and the offense.

I was angry, mad, and hurt that I had to deal with the shame and history, but the Bible says the truth sets us free. I am thankful there is no condemnation for those who are in Christ Jesus. When I left from that house that day, I was free. I released that man from my judgment. I drove away with no shame, no fear, and no guilt. I was confident and sure of who I was in Christ.

There came a day when the abuser died in a tragic accident while riding a bicycle in the city. In a way, I was relieved when I heard about his death because now I knew he would never abuse another child.

I often hear men justify their behavior because they are men. If women were to behave in the same way, they would be labeled. The inequality is wrong. Both men and women are created in the image of God for His purpose and His glory. Not one of us is justified in abusing others. We are all held to the same standard in God's eyes.

I applaud women such as the fearless trailblazers, Harriet Tubman, Michelle Obama, Sojourner Truth, and many others. They are women who fought for freedom, and the rights of the oppressed and the enslaved. These women dared to dream. My respect is not limited to the political world. Women of God, authors, and speakers like Beth Moore and Joyce Meyer, have paved the way for someone like me to be a difference-maker in the Christian community.

I am learning to speak openly and honestly about the impact of violence against women. The hands of boys and men have unjustly mistreated women for too long. Many of us give so much of ourselves to men and receive so much hurt in return. The spirit of the woman needs liberation from fear, and deliverance from enslavement to the chains of injustice. There is a world full of hurting women who struggle, just like I struggled, to find freedom from prison cells of emotional entrapment. We must help each other.

I Have Overcome

I have wanted to write a book about my life for a long time. Some wonder, why now? Why write a book about the pain in your life after accomplishing such great successes? The doubts in my head tell me not to write about my pain. The doubts tell me to let the idea go and to keep the pain buried deep inside. My intuition tells me that I must write my story to heal fully. I must expose the lies I was told, and the lies I have lived.

Reading other people's stories and how they have dealt with their life has not been enough to free me. It's my turn to dig deeper and discover the "why" and "how" of my life.

Chapter 7 • Chains are Broken

Why? Why do I do what I do? Why do I feel what I feel? What drives me? How will God use me for His glory?

My search for significance is real. The process of putting it all on paper is not easy for me. Sitting here at my laptop recounting all I've lost is not easy. So, I will grind, I will work, I will think. How will my story bring clarity to readers? How will my work add value to other's lives? Until I regain what was stolen from me, I will not break free from the cycles of indecision, broken relationships, meanness, and other haunting terrors that invade the inner most being of my soul.

Perhaps shining light into the dark places of my life will allow me to discover what went wrong. Maybe the light will push me to use the power of creativity in me, which I covered for so long with an insatiable desire for education. Like a mask, formal education blocked the real work God wanted to do in me for a long time.

I used masks to cover the truth of the shame left behind in my spirit. I've worn masks of success, and of being a fierce girl and a strong woman. A poem by Paul Laurence Dunbar describes how we hide our true selves behind masks.

> *We wear the mask that grins and lies,*
> *it hides our cheeks and shades our eyes, —*
> *this debt we pay to human guile;*
> *with torn and bleeding hearts we smile,*
> *and mouth with myriad subtleties.*

Why should the world be over-wise,
in counting all our tears and sighs?
Nay, let them only see us, while
we wear the mask.
We smile, but, O great Christ, our cries
to thee from tortured souls arise.
We sing, but oh the clay is vile
beneath our feet, and long the mile;
but let the world dream otherwise,
we wear the mask!

Lessons Learned

I sought freedom, and now I am ready to share my story. It is a story of defeat, of victory, of shame, of wanting to give up. It is a story of wanting to walk off the face of the world, or at least to hide in the furthest corner away from everyone. I no longer have anything left to prove to the world. Now it's just God and me. This is my journey. It is my story to tell. I dig deep past my pain to discover the real me—the me God created before the traps of Satan damaged me. Satan desired to sift me like wheat, to shred me to pieces, to yield me ineffective, null and void. But here I am writing a book. I'm writing about my heart, my messed-up life, and how I have overcome. Do not be afraid to face your problems. Through it all, I learned how to rely on God. I learned how to stand alone. I learned how to release pain and how to forgive. Nothing can prevent the will of God from happening in my life. There are no weapons that are formed against me that will prosper (Isaiah 54:17). I made it so can you.

As a woman, I have learned to pull my head up and to believe in myself. I believe in the abilities God has given me, and I will not be denied or oppressed by the negativity of evil people. Encounters with evil and wickedness are very real, but I am unafraid because I trust in the LORD my God.

As I have stumbled through the darkness, I have learned God saw me through it all. If He did it before, He will do it again. If it had not been for the Lord, I don't know where I would be today. I am thankful that God found me and He saved me. He will do it again. God will always be with me through every low valley and high mountain. He did not give me the "spirit of fear; but of power, and of love, and of a sound mind" (2 Timothy 1:7).

Application

Let go of strong feelings connected to the past. Guilt and shame are only designed to kill you and keep you bound. They will hinder your destiny. God is taking you somewhere, and He wants you to release all the baggage from the past.

Don't live in fear. Live in freedom so that you can fulfill all the promises of God. He has so many promises right here for you.

Wholeness and forgiveness will bring the joy and happiness you long for. Forgive those who have caused the trauma. Forgive yourself and release yourself from shame. Work on yourself every day by showing self-love and imagining better days. You will find joy and happiness again. It will happen, but you must take one day at a time.

God is on your side. Look to Him to walk with you and hold your hand. Lean on Him every step of the way. You can do it.

Questions

1. Is childhood pain blocking you from moving forward into God's plan for your life?

2. Have you had to fight for your personal sense of worth? What damaged or stole your sense of worth from you?

3. What can you do to increase your sense of wholeness?

4. Have you practiced releasing yourself from pain through forgiveness?

5. How can you empower the women around you who are struggling to build confidence and break free from emotional bondage?

6. Do a personal inventory to examine any areas of your life that you need God to heal? Put it before God and ask Him to show you the way.

chapter 8
Jealousy

*The heart is deceitful above all things and beyond cure.
Who can understand it?*

Jeremiah 17:9

It was Monday morning after a long, boring weekend sitting in the house, going outside in the early fall weather, and going back in again. It seemed Monday would never arrive, but once it did, I had to face reality again.

I watched them walking down the school hallway. She giggled as he wrapped his arm around her waist. Each time I saw them, my heart burned with jealousy that I was no longer his girl.

The day-by-day scene hurt my heart. At night, I would lie on my bed and cry in pain, only to see them happy again the next day. My broken heart hurt so bad, and I did not know how to process the pain. I do not think I've ever truly dealt with the pain of lost love, which became the source of my jealousy.

The Beginning of Jealousy
The Hebrew word for "jealous" is translated as "zealous." The word is used in the Old Testament to describe God as

being "jealous or zealous" for His people. God's love burns for His people, and He does not want anything or anyone to come between them and His love. God's love for us is on fire.

The godly definition of "jealousy" denotes sincerity and purity. Jealousy is attached to an indescribable emotion that wells up inside of the heart and overflows logic. Jealousy consumes the heart and leads to uncharacteristic behavior.

God's jealousy is pure, but sinful humanity corrupts emotion. The human side of jealousy lends itself to mean and hateful behavior. In this chapter, I discuss the human kind of jealousy that festers and grows into grudges and revenge. Jealousy hides behind false smiles, tight hugs, and well wishes. Jealousy creeps its ugly head in homes, churches, the workplace, and anywhere we go. Maybe it's seeing someone succeed in life that causes jealousy. Maybe it's seeing their happy relationships filled with smiles, laughter, and real love.

The devil was envious of God for creating such a perfect earth, with perfect people. Jealousy fueled Satan's desire to permanently destroy the earth. Isn't that's what jealousy does? It seeks to destroy, tear down, and annihilate the happiness of others. Jealousy seems to say, "I'm miserable, so let me see how I can make you just as miserable as I am." Jealousy conveys the desire to see another person hurt. It has a mission to destroy, ruin, and secretly plot to injure another. Sinful jealousy comes from the evil heart of the devil.

Jealousy and envy do not appear in a person all of sudden, but rather they fester and seethe, developing over time. It starts out as a small seed of "humph" and then snowballs into an evil monster. Once jealousy is out of control, its deep roots enter into the heart and take control of the mind, the will, and the emotions.

Jealous tendencies stem back as far as Adam and Eve's children. The story of Cain and Abel is an example of an incredible saga of jealousy and envy. Cain couldn't stand the fact that Abel had a better sacrifice than he did. His jealousy and envy grew so strong it eventually led him to murder his brother in a field.

I believe Cain did not start out hating his beloved brother, but as time passed something in their relationship began to change. Abel's prosperity caused Cain too much pain. The sacrifices he made bothered Cain. His brother gave too much, put too much heart into his work for God. Cain watched with jealousy and could not stand the fact God accepted Abel's sacrifices, but not his.

Often, a person develops jealousy and envy because they feel uncelebrated, unappreciated, and devalued. I wonder if Cain felt his efforts were unappreciated as God smiled on Abel's sacrifices but frowned on Cain's. As jealousy reared its ugly head, Cain plotted ways to annihilate the pain in his heart. He would go after what he thought was the source of his pain. In reality, Cain was not angry with Abel, but with God.

Genesis is the book of beginnings, and so it chronicles the beginning of the destruction of mankind. Destruction started with the devil creating mistrust within an otherwise healthy relationship. Once the devil sowed seeds of jealousy and envy, the sinful nature took over with mistrust, insecurity, and pride.

Thankfully, God had another plan, and the devil's plan for destruction did not work. Evil did not prevail. Grace and mercy prevailed and still does. God looked beyond the heart of man and showed compassion on the creatures He created.

I Have Overcome

From the outside, it would not seem I possessed low self-esteem. I was not born with a sign that said, "Pick on her. She's not worthy. She's just *this*, or she's just *that*." Still, others degraded me, talked about me, and criticized me just for being myself.

"She smiles too much and is always grinning."

Well, what's wrong with that? Why ridicule someone because they are happy and carry a joyful spirit? Some people make it hard for you to be you and put pressure on you to act and be like someone else.

My struggle came from the people who were supposed to nurture, support, and love me. They were supposed to be kind but were the most critical and judgmental. I now realize where the source of a lot of my pain came from. It came from the treatment I received from older people in my life jealous of the beautiful little girl full of confidence, hope, and resilience.

Because I did not think much of myself, I let others walk over me and use me as the proverbial doormat to wipe the feet. Moving on is a great challenge for a person who has a heart cemented in the past.

Exposed is the lie that any of us has our lives together. Some of our sins have been put on public display, and others are still in the closet tucked secretly away in hopes that no one will ever open the door. We barricade our secrets to keep anyone from finding out the real person behind the happy smiling face.

To live is to have personal struggles. The one who never struggles with a personal issue is the one who does not need God in their lives. I have struggled most of my life. Now it's time to live in the spirit realm, to go where God wants me to be. There is no limit to where the Spirit of God can take me.

Lessons Learned

The heart is a powerful instrument. It can hold deep love, but it can also hold deep jealousies, envy, and hate. I have known relationships to crumble because of jealousy brooding, festering, and exploding torrential damage into a once healthy relationship. Once jealousy overtakes trust, it is hard to recover. Love dies, and the relationship dies. Jealousy has done its dirty work and destroyed the relationship.

The pure heart turned jealous starts to imagine evil. Good intentions turn to bad. The thought of celebrating another person's success seems so far away. How could I possibly celebrate someone else's job promotion or ministry success when everything I do goes uncelebrated?

It is unfortunate that some people do not like to see others happy, prospering and enjoying the abundant life. Because their lives are so miserable and messed up, some people are offended as they watch others contentedly carry on successfully. I don't want to be that kind of person. I want to be the kind of person who knows there is room for everyone to succeed.

Application

How can we avoid ending up like Cain, driven away with a curse? What is the solution to the jealousy problem? I wish I could tell you a simple solution, but I don't have all the answers. I am only recounting seasons of my heart to capture the root of pain and deliverance from the lies I believed.

Writing is my process of healing. I want to be free. I am on a journey to escape the prison cells locking me up, the iron bars that block me from being the person I was meant to be. I am reaching out to let you know that you too can push through your personal struggles, even as I am right now growing and becoming the woman God called me to be. None of us have arrived. All of life is a journey.

We've all been impacted by jealousy in one form or another. You may or may not struggle with jealousy, but you have some kind of struggle. Perhaps your struggle came from the way jealous people treated you. Or maybe you are the one treating others poorly because of what you perceive their life to be.

The mind and the heart are delicate. Tread lightly when talking to people. Be considerate of others and do not think it does not leave lasting harm. Find your own purpose instead of tearing others down. Spend time examining your own story.

Questions

1. Have you ever felt jealous of someone? What were you jealous over? Was your jealousy pure like God's, or corrupt and destructive like the devil's?

2. Have you ever been mistreated because someone else was jealous of you?

3. There is an old quote that says, "Jealousy is as cruel as the grave." To deal with the pain of poor treatment due to another person's jealousy, remember what it was like when you felt jealous of someone else. Gather compassion for the person who is jealous of you. Try to consider where their pain comes from. It doesn't justify their behavior toward you, but it will help you to forgive them and move out of your pain.

chapter 9
Relinquishing Control

Trust in the Lord with all your heart, and do not lean on your own understanding. In all your ways acknowledge him, and he will make straight your paths.
Proverbs 3:5-6 ESV

The years passed by, and I was no longer a silly fifteen-year-old stumbling around from relationship to relationship. I became a fully-grown woman in a very bad relationship, but the jealousy in my heart was still there.

Possession and envy permeated my thoughts. Disdain for the one I claimed to love developed in my heart because he would not conform to my wishes. We argued, fought, and experienced horrifying Friday nights. Some of those nights included my husband's gang of friends. They clustered in the kitchen. I never went back there and had no idea what was going on.

As I look back and think about the residue left behind, the aluminum foil and the pot on the stove, I realize it was the evidence of drug abuse. I now realize what really was happening in the back of the house. Thank God, I never was curious to know what he and his friends were doing, and I never touched any kinds of drugs. God had a purpose for my life, and He protected and preserved me from what could have been an even worse situation.

About a week before, I stumbled into a Methodist church. At only twenty-years-old, my life was lost, and I had no hope of it improving. My eyes filled with tears from the pain in my head and body as I sat in the pew. Earlier that day, I was slammed against a dresser and hit on the side of the head.

I cried out to the God of my youth, asking Him to help me out of the life I was in. Not knowing the next move to make, I returned home to try to make some kind of sense out of my situation. Walking out that church that Sunday afternoon would lead to a turnaround situation. I stopped by my sister's house to visit for a while and headed for the walk back home.

When I returned home that day, my husband had left the house and taken the car, all of my jewelry, and all of the money. He was just gone.

With no car, I had no transportation for work, and it was a cold February. The next week I woke up at four a.m., got dressed, and walked to work at McDonald's. I remember bundling up in my white winter coat to head across the tracks in the bitter cold.

That week was hard and rough, but I walked into work still with a smile on my face. There was something on the inside of me that just would not allow me to give up. I kept pushing, and I kept smiling, not knowing what my future would hold.

I held onto a hope inside of me that said if I keep going to school and working hard things would get better for me. God showed His favor to me in so many ways, but yet still in so many ways, I always felt alone. Thankfully, God had a plan to show me I was not alone.

Lessons Learned

In this world, we will face times of extreme joy and times of extreme trials and tribulations. The hard work comes in navigating life in such a way where we don't lose our minds trying to be everything to everybody. We have enough to work through focusing on ourselves. Undue stress, sickness, and various disease can result from trying to solve OPP (Other People's Problems). There are some things we cannot change. In particular, we cannot change people. I learned that with my husband. There was nothing I could do to change him.

In 1941, Reinhold Niebuhr (1892-1971) penned the Serenity Prayer. The prayer-poem helped me learn to let go of the people and situations that were impacting my life in a negative way. I hope it encourages you as well.

> *God grant me the serenity*
> *to accept the things I cannot change;*
> *courage to change the things I can;*
> *and wisdom to know the difference.*

Living one day at a time;
enjoying one moment at a time;
accepting hardships as the pathway to peace;
taking, as He did, this sinful world
as it is, not as I would have it;
trusting that He will make all things right
if I surrender to His Will;
that I may be reasonably happy in this life
and supremely happy with Him
forever in the next.
Amen.

Application

The Bible says we each must work out our own salvation with fear and trembling. A person must make up his or her mind to change, or change will not happen. We have to be responsible for the areas of our own lives that need changing. We must take hold of courage to make changes to our negative thought patterns by putting the Word of God into our minds. We renew our minds by the Word of God, saturating our hearts in what is good, pure, and honest.

Seek God for the right relationships. Ask God to heal you from past abuses and hurts. Follow hard after God, disassociate yourself from the negative, cut away toxic relationships, and cultivate the positive friendships that lift you higher. Don't allow yourself to be a victim of your circumstance or a product of your environment.

We are each responsible for our actions. The Bible tells us "we shall reap what we sow." Whatever we put into the ground, the harvest of that seed will multiple in our lives. When we see the manifestation of love, or hate, emerging in our lives, it should come as no surprise because that is what we planted.

The more we embrace the reality that we are not God, the more peace we will have. We are not in control; God is in control. We are not omnipresent, omnipotent, or omniscient, but God is. The more we place our lives in God's hand, the clearer our purpose will become. Turn your life and problems over to Jesus, and let Him work it out. Let go of the handlebars of life, and trust God. God wants us to live in His presence knowing with full assurance that He cares for us.

Questions

1. Is there a circumstance or person in your life that throws you off balance and causes you to fret? Do you constantly think about that circumstance or person, and try to change it?

2. Instead of focusing on the areas of life we cannot control, we must focus instead on what we can control. What area of your life is in your control that you can shift your focus to?

3. Ultimately, we have control over our choices and reaction to circumstances, but other than that, there is very little in life we do control. Write about the peace of mind you feel knowing that God loves you and wants the best for your life, even in the midst of circumstances that seem out of control.

chapter 10
Tragedy Struck at Midnight

The day of the Lord's return will come unexpectedly, like a thief in the night.
1 Thessalonians 5:2 NIV

It was at midnight on a Saturday night when I heard a brisk knock on the front door. It startled me as I lay on the couch, still waiting for my husband to come home. A week had passed since he left.

"Who is it?" I asked.

It was the police. I answered the door, and the man on the other side of the screen told me my husband was in a bad car accident and they didn't expect him to live.

It was a bad wreck. Lester was thrown out of the car and suffered a terrible neck break. A car rolled over on him and crushed many other parts of his body. The other people involved in the crash walked away unscathed.

Without hesitation, I ran out the door to find a ride to Savannah. I had not had a car all week, so I walked up the road to Miss Viola's house. Someone gave me a ride to the hospital in Savannah, and when I arrived, the doctors came out with more bad news. My husband was paralyzed from the neck down and would never be able to walk again.

I crumbled to my knees as the news hit my ears. Confusion pierced through my body like a sharp knife. What exactly did all of this mean? I was a young girl with little knowledge of the medical arena. It just didn't make sense. I was in shock.

So, there I was, sitting by his side in the hospital, dozing off from the sound of the respirator lulling me to sleep. The sterile air in the room was frigid and still. My whole life changed from fighting and struggling to survive, to nothing really matters except hoping he heals and gets better.

It didn't matter that the house was left unattended. It didn't matter that I would not go back to work. It didn't matter where my next meal would come from. All that mattered to me was for my husband to would get better and come home. Little did I know that God Himself had a hand in the accident. God was guiding my life.

The late-night news marked a new beginning for me. It was definite game-changer. I didn't know the whirlwind of change that was about to come in my life. I have no doubt that God Himself orchestrated the occurrences at that hospital. The timing was synchronized perfectly and every single need, both physical and spiritual, was met.

My faith grew as I met God at that hospital. God visited me one night in my dream, and I was left with the feeling that angels carried all of my problems away. I felt assurance all was well, and God would take care of me. So, the journey began. From those moments on, I felt a heavy load had lifted from my shoulders. The load of sin, guilt, and shame I carried around so long was gone. Before that time in my life, I had the self-esteem of a petunia—none. I felt lower than the lowest valley. Now I felt light. I could smile. I could hold my head up.

A Jewish woman and her husband were riding in the same elevator as me. The woman offered to pray for me as she saw me struggling in pain. As she said my name before God, the Holy Spirit entered into my body, and I felt His strength. It was as if I was on cloud nine, and filled with such lightness. Every ounce of guilt and shame lifted from me. The joy I experienced was unspeakable. God's peace and serenity gave me confidence that everything was going to be alright.

The experience seemed more like an angelic visitation ministering to me than a random woman in an elevator. I shall forever remember those moments as I go through this life. God knew exactly what I needed, and He saved by the blood of Jesus. He forgave all of my sins and took away the heaviness, and the weight of the guilt and the shame I had carried all of my life to that point.

I did not leave the hospital. I had no clothes, no money, no food, and no family with—just me by myself. I had nowhere to take a bath and no change of clothes, so I was beginning to stink, and I was hungry. Some days I ate, and some days I did not.

My husband was still in a coma. Every day I would go to his bedside and beg him to just open his eyes, squeeze my hand, wiggle a toe, anything to give me a sign that he would come through this situation.

I met a lot of people who came through the hospital waiting room, who were going through trials. I felt the hand of God in every situation.

Ms. Tilletha Thomaston and her family were angels sent from above. She came to the waiting room after her brother had an aneurysm. She took me under her wing just as a mother would a daughter. She invited me into her home, fed me, and bought me clothes. I was a complete stranger to her, but she and her family treated me like one of her own family members.

In the Psalms 68:6, it says God places the lonely in families. That's what God did for me. He placed me, a lost child, in beautiful and loving families.

My trust was only in God. My parents and brothers and sisters had no resources to share with me. They had very limited finances to care for their own. They did not have money to help me during the tremendous losses I experienced.

The question still rings in my mind, "Where would I be if it had not been for the LORD?" I cannot say where I would be, but I am grateful God loved me enough not to leave me alone. God took care of me during the most tremendous loss of my life. I was in Savannah all alone with no job and no income, but God placed me into a loving family. I stayed in touch with the Thomaston family for many years.

Chapter 10 • Tragedy Struck at Midnight

Transferred

Eventually, my husband recovered enough, and the hospital decided to transfer him to Shepherd Spinal Clinic, a few hours away in Atlanta. The transfer wasn't an easy transition. The ride was very bumpy, and he had to lay in traction.

The nurses at Shepherd Spinal Clinic were the most caring and compassionate human beings I have ever encountered. At first, my husband was on a unit with several patients in one room. The other patients inspired me as I watched them regain their strength. We stayed at Shepherd Spinal Center from February to August.

It's amazing how God made the human spirit to withstand so much pain, so much tragedy, and so much hurt. The men and women at the clinic were full of resiliency as they readjusted to life in a wheelchair and relearned how to walk and how to talk.

The families of those men and women also possessed strength beyond human comprehension. Life comes with many challenges, but God supplies every one of us with the tenacity to overcome the most difficult circumstances. If it had not been for God making a way out of no way, and putting the right people in place in my life, I don't know where I would be today. God saw me through each and every step of the way.

There I was in the city of Atlanta with no money and no help, just sitting in the waiting room with other families experiencing similar circumstances. At night, I slept in the gym area on a mat with a little blanket one of the nurses provided to me.

I don't know how the way was made, but one evening a man named Mr. Lamb came by the hospital and told me I could come to his home and stay with his family.

At first, I was afraid. How was I going to get back to the hospital? I didn't really want to leave Lester's side. I had already left everything else in my life. I left my home. I left my job. I left everything to be there with my husband. Nothing else mattered to me except him getting better.

The host family I stayed with was a very large family with strong Christian values. It was the first time I witnessed a family functioning properly. The circumstances which brought me into this positive atmosphere happened in a sudden and abrupt tragic manner, but God had a plan to broaden my perspective.

Fear

Despite knowing God was with me, fear was one of my daily companions. There were some days I had no resources and depended solely on the family I was living with. They were gracious, but I knew they were tired of me eating their groceries and using their gas. So eventually, I got a job at the cafeteria of the Piedmont Hospital in Atlanta.

The first night I walked to the bus stop to go home was interesting. I was in Atlanta, with no transportation, trying

Chapter 10 • Tragedy Struck at Midnight

to find my way. I took the bus as far as I could go and walked the rest of the way to the Lamb's house. I was oblivious to the potential dangers that existed in Atlanta. God watched over me and protected me from all danger.

My testimony during that time may seem simple or trivial to many, but for me, it was as if I was a lost sheep and Jesus was my Shepherd. He led me through the valley of the shadow of death. I didn't need to fear evil. I just followed His voice.

Once I was lost at the Marta train station and a man with a snow-white face dressed in all black approached me gave me concise, succinct directions without me even asking. I have no doubt the man was an angel God sent to help me find my way. There were many other miraculous occurrences throughout those days. God was increasing my faith by leaps and bounds.

People would give me money for no apparent reason. All of my needs were met. As I write this, I am reflecting on the mighty hand of God. He never left me, and He never allowed me to go a day without eating or having a place to lay my head.

Psalm 23:4 says, "Yea, though I walk through the valley of the shadow of death, I will fear no evil; For You are with me; your rod and your staff, they comfort me." This verse came alive to me during the dark valley days of my life. All I could do was take one day at a time, walking and trusting God every step of the way. No matter what situation you find yourself in God will be with you through it. You just have to follow hard after Him and keep your eyes on of Him.

Romans 8:28 says, "All things work together for the good of those who love God and are the called according to His purpose." This verse played out in my life in a real way. Through all of the tragedy, I grew in my relationship with God.

After I gave my life to God at the hospital in Savannah, it seemed as if God orchestrated people into my life to impact me in a major way. I had no control over what was happening to me, but God was in control.

My experience in Atlanta drew me into a higher perspective of life. God planted me among loving and nurturing people. Along with the Lamb family, I will never forget the kindness Ms. Ponder showed me. She owned a dry-cleaning business in the community and attended the same church the Lambs went to.

Some days, Ms. Ponder would unexpectedly hand me money. She invited me into her home for Bible Study. She allowed me to sit at her dry-cleaners on Tuesdays while I waited for the bus to pick me up. She gave me rides to and from the Lamb's house to the hospital. I do not have the words to explain how much I appreciated her.

The favor I received at Berean Bible Baptist Church was as amazing to me as the kindness of the Christian family, the Thomastons, I met at St. Joseph's Hospital in Savannah. I am so thankful I know God is real. He showed me just how much He loved me when I was completely at the bottom.

Chapter 10 • Tragedy Struck at Midnight

God provides for His children, especially when we run out of resources. I ran out of resources, but God took over and provided every one of my needs. He provided the love I needed, the shelter I needed, the food I needed, and spiritual training I needed. There is a song called *Indescribable,* by Keira Sheared. That song sums up how God took care to make sure the right people were in place at the right times to help in my time of need.

If it had not been for the LORD on my side, I tremble to imagine where I would be. The lesson in all this is to recognize that God is at work and we must relinquish control of our lives. God will take care of us, but we must surrender control to Him. Consciously letting go gives God controlling power over our lives.

I remembered the Sunday I walked into the Methodist Church and prayed for God to change my life because it was headed in a horrible direction. I called out to the God of my youth who had stayed with me through every situation. I didn't pray for God to allow my husband to be in a bad accident. I didn't pray to be placed in a strange place, dependent on strangers. But that is the way God led my life, and He continued to guide me even when I did ask for His guidance. He pulled me into His plan for my life.

Lessons Learned

Having nothing taught me how utterly dependent I was on God to provide for me. I would not know and love God the way I do now if I had not experienced Him providing my daily bread. I did not know one day to the next how I would eat, where I would sleep, how I would take a bath, or where my next dollar would come from. God provided everything I needed.

That experience taught me that when I was down to nothing, God was up to something in me. He showed me His Hand. He revealed to me His Son Jesus. He drew so close to me, and His presence was so real.

I learned first-hand that God is real. God's closeness to me during those trying months meant more to me than anything I experienced in all of my life. The most powerful lesson I learned was to rest in God and love Him first. The Bible tells us to seek first the kingdom of God and His righteousness, and all these things will be added to you.

Application

When faced with an uncertain, seemingly hopeless situation, try not to control everything with your own solutions. It is better to wait on God to work it out in His way. Spend time reading your Bible and praying. God answers in His way. Stay humble and trust the ways of God.

God does not work how we think He will. God is all powerful and does things the way He chooses. He is God all by Himself and has no limit to His power. God is full of all power, all wisdom, and all provision.

Chapter 10 • Tragedy Struck at Midnight

Questions

1. Have you ever experienced an unexpected tragedy that left you feeling hopeless?

2. Did anything happen in the midst of your pain that allowed you to feel God's presence and provision?

3. If you are going through tragedy now, surround yourself with people who care about you. Turn to God if you don't have people in your life that care, or even if they do care, but do not have the capacity to help you. God cares, and He will put people in your life to help you. Accept their help, and thank God for His provision.

chapter 11
From Fear to Faith

*God has not given us a spirit of fear,
but of power and of love and of a sound mind.*
2 Timothy 1:7 NKJV

For a long time, the dreary and dark feelings that emerged from the thoughts of my soul tore me apart. My heart felt ripped up, and my face as if it might fall off. The heaviness came from multiple layers of depth within me.

I had to learn to peel back the layers and layers of hurt and pain that were covered up. At times, my mind would sink so low only God could lift my head as I read His Word.

I would pray for the chains to break, and the fetters to be loosed. As I prayed, I clinched my teeth, and my fists, begging for God to uproot the bitterness and the pain that had grown deep down inside. I struggled with letting go of the memories and releasing the people who hurt me. I knew I have to forgive to move on, but it was a tough process.

Over time and through prayer, a lifting took place. The sadness lessened, and the terror of worthlessness decreased. Even in the face of the darkest trials, I had to continue pressing through because I knew one day it would be better. It would not always be so painful.

God built my faith through the valley of the shadow of death and through experiencing tremendous loss. Every loss I experienced gave me something spiritual to gain. I relied on my faith in God to wake me up every day, whether I felt like it or not.

One may ask, what is faith? Faith to me is like an exchange. I exchange what I hold in my hand for something I cannot see in God's hand. I make the exchange because I know the hand of God has something for me that is far more valuable than what I have to offer Him. What He gives to me will add value to my life.

Walking in faith requires letting go of all you depended on before God. The truth was, I really didn't have much to cling to before I met God, except my limited intellect and the outward beauty I was blessed with. And then I had hurt, pain, and tragedy.

The fear I had inside is now gone. I exchanged it for God's peace. The grimy memories of empty promises and the lies that troubled my mind have been relegated to the past. What happened yesterday does not impact my today because today I have another chance to triumph in faith.

My faith walk was not anything that I sought out. In a way, it developed out of desperation, but in time divinely pushed me into my destiny and purpose. When I gave my life to God, I had no idea I would one day be where I am today. Sometimes I find myself lost in thought, and wondering how I came to where I am today, especially when

Chapter 11 · From Fear to Faith

I find myself sitting at the table with voices of power and influence.

How did a country-raised girl, with a low self-esteem, full of fear, and with seemingly limited talent end up as a Ph.D. graduate in ministry? I attribute my successes to the grace of God. God's grace leads me and gives me the strength to do what I do. I truly "can do all things through Christ who gives me strength" (Philippians 4:13).

My breakthrough points (I say points because there have been more than one breakthrough point in my life) continued to propel me forward. My first breakthrough happened when I came to the knowledge that no one really cared about what I did, so I might as well go after my dreams.

When I stopped waiting for others to approve of me is when I started making plans for my life. My education birthed from that breakthrough. I decided just to do what I wanted to because if I didn't go after my dreams, no one else would go after them for me.

Another breakthrough moment of revelation came from a book I read about mapping out life. When I took up the reins of my life, it began to take on a shape that made sense to me. No one can order and plan my life for me. I must think for myself, and develop a master plan in sync with God's divine purpose for my life. I began to believe that limitless possibilities lie within this lump of clay.

None of us know what we are capable of unless we take a leap of faith. In order for the car to start, we have to take action and turn the key. Too often we do not take chances on ourselves. Taking a chance on your ability may perhaps take you to places you never thought you could go.

I am taking a chance on myself by writing this book. I am jumping, taking a big leap of faith. Even if no one ever picks up this book to read it, I have faith that if I bear my soul in it, something much more valuable in the Spirit will come to me. It's easy to hide how we truly feel, but exposing the truth takes courage.

My life is not only for me but for the many other young women who came from obscurity to emerge as champions. I'm living proof that it is possible to come up out of bad circumstances, and become whatever you want to be.

Lessons Learned

When a person is born, there is a not a price tag that limits their worth and value. God does not value one life more than another. Where then does each person's potential come from?

What factors lead one person to become a millionaire and another person to be content on welfare? Where did the root of poverty come from and why does it impact the human existence to the degree it does? Isn't all life worthy of love and does not all life have value and meaning?

For a long time, I framed life in an unrealistic way. I cared too much of what others thought of me. One day, I received some great advice from a wise person. "Always be yourself and don't try to be like no one else. Stay to yourself, remain humble, and you will go far." I took that advice to heart.

There will always be pressure to be like others, to make everybody happy, and to make everybody like you. The fact of the matter is, everyone will not like you or be happy for you. Sure, some show a little care about your accomplishments, but the reality of it is no one really cares you just received a promotion or earned a Ph.D. Most everyone is working on achieving their own life goals and dreams to really care about the next person.

Their biggest concern is always, "How does your achievement impact my goals and dreams?" If there is no connection, they simply toss your accomplishments to the side. Some people only want to be associated with your success to leverage their own road toward success. Live for God, and God alone. His view toward me is the only pure view with no ulterior motives. His love has no ulterior motive.

Letting go of the opinions and evaluations of others is liberating! Our peace of mind depends greatly on what we meditate upon. The more the mind dwells on other people and their opinion, the more it sinks deeper into negativity. God tells us to meditate on His Word day and night. He will keep us in perfect peace as we concentrate our minds on Him.

Application

Our lives are often a reflection of our experiences. Our experiences impact the way we do life, whether we push forward in victory, or allow ourselves to wallow in self-defeat. It takes time to remove yourself from everything that has influenced you, to find the true you God created you to be.

Go on a conquest to discover what makes you tick. Get to know yourself. You have done so much for everyone else; now it's time to do some self-discovery. Discover things about yourself by thinking about what brings you joy and what drives you to succeed.

One thing I know about myself is that music makes me feel good. I know I don't perform at peak levels when I am physically tired. I need time to sit and to think. I work better in places of calm and quiet.

As you learn about your preferences and what makes you happy, you will be able to surround yourself with an atmosphere that brings out the best in you. When you feel comfortable and safe, you will be able to separate yourself from fear and begin to open your heart to God.

Life can be a challenge for all of us, but when we find our place in God, He can move us from fear to faith. God has a purpose beyond your pain and heartache. Allow Him to heal you and to reveal His plan for your unique life.

Questions

1. What have been the most defining moments of your life thus far? Maybe it was the way you grew up or overcoming a tragedy that occurred, or an accomplishment that helped you define who you are.

2. What words of wisdom have you learned in your breakthrough moments? What truths have set you free from the fear in your life?

3. Do you have a safe space where you can be the real you with God? Where is it? Do you have people in your life that love you just as you are as well as encourage you to grow? Who is speaking positive over your life? If no one else is, commit to speak positive over your own life.

chapter 12
Flawed, but Called

*To this he called you . . . that you may
obtain the glory of our Lord Jesus Christ.*
2 Thessalonians 2:14 ESV

From early on in my life, I was a quiet one who kept to herself. I never tried to lead anyone while I was in high school or college. Once the Lord saved me, leadership qualities began to emerge in my life, surprising me. All of this occurred during my marriage to Lester, as I was caring for him.

Beginning in the winter of 1989, my life took a complete turnaround. God was serious when He put His Hand on my life. Before that point, I knew little of the Bible and could not even understand it if I tried to read it. It was a foreign book to me. I would read, and it just did not make sense.

One winter night, I had a supernatural experience as I was sleeping in my bed. I had just come home from the hospital in Savannah where my husband was receiving therapy. The experience I had was a mystical dream. It was surreal. God's Spirit fell upon my body, and I was never the same again. He lifted me above my problems, and it felt as if I was walking on clouds. It was such a full experience. God gave me what I needed during the roughest and darkest days of my life. I am convinced that He was carrying me through.

I began to teach Sunday school and Bible studies. I submerged myself reading books on leadership. The Leader who inspired me above them all is Jesus, of course. The gospel of John provided me with the perfect model of a great leader. Jesus went about serving others, healing others, and giving to others, without ever expecting recognition or acknowledgment.

At the wedding feast, Jesus fixed the problem when the hosts ran out of wine. His mother encouraged Him because she knew He was the greatest leader among them. Jesus did as He was asked, selflessly. He shows His stable character of servanthood over and over in the Gospels.

My first role ever as a "leader" was teaching Sunday school to white girls at the First Baptist Church in Vidalia. That experience taught me so much about teaching and having influence. At that time, I knew nothing about teaching, but the leaders of that church entrusted me to teach those young children.

I love those kids, and they loved me. There was never any prejudice at all. They did not see me as black, they saw me as their Sunday school teacher. One experience that stands out in my mind is the day I packed all of the girls in my little Volkswagen Jetta and took them out for breakfast.

One summer, all of us who served in youth ministry attended a youth retreat with the kids at Lake Sinclair in

Chapter 12 • Flawed, but Called | 109

Milledgeville, Georgia. It was a wonderful experience of learning to spend quiet time with God and connecting with the girls in a real and personal way.

I learned as much as the girls did about living life to its fullest. The retreat experience was so rich in building relationships with each other, and in digging deeper into our relationship with God.

It was a lot of fun too! I learned how to swim and how to ride a jet ski. I worked with a wonderful group of other youth leaders. Not only did that one experience enrich my life, but as a group, we would often go out on various outings, like to Pizza Hut, and to other churches' youth conferences. My experiences transferred into other areas of my life and future ministries.

Ministry means a great deal to me because its where I discovered my purpose in life. When I gave my life to Jesus and was born again, God planted a fire inside my heart. The fire of the Holy Ghost ignited such a hunger and thirst for knowledge I began to saturate myself in the Bible and other Christian self-help literature. During that season of my life, I experienced exponential growth and development on so many levels.

My experience reminds me of the poem "Footprints in the Sand," which gives me a vivid image of God carrying me on the beach of life. All of my experiences could have taken me in a bad direction, but instead, God led me to Himself through the hard times.

God used my life to lead me to faith in Him, to a relationship with Him, and to serve in ministry. At one point, I did have the audacity to look back. I made some mistakes and wrong choices. I thank God He gave me a second opportunity to recommit my soul to Him, lest I die in my sins.

God is a forgiving God. His love endures forever. He never gave up on me. Certainly, I had those who hated me, who turned their backs on me, and who spoke badly of me, but God never did any of those things to me. God has never left me. He has never written me off as unusable. He continues to amaze me.

Lessons Learned

Some argue leaders are born; some argue leaders are made. Neither view is right or wrong. Some people are born with leadership qualities that simply need honed, sculptured, and developed. Other people are born with seemingly no leadership capabilities, but once they are given an opportunity to lead, the individual works diligently in integrity and with love.

I propose that the leader among us is the one everybody goes to for solutions to their problems. The true leader is the kind of person who gives their shoulder for others to cry on. The true leader is a doer. The leader doesn't waste time wishing and wanting but gets to work right away.

Chapter 12 • Flawed, but Called

An influential leader is one who is decisive and sure, who can move forward deliberately. Jesus never asked, "Should we feed these people? Let's form a committee to decide if we should help these people." Jesus saw what needed to be done and immediately met the need.

Poor leaders lack integrity as he or she will say one thing, and do another. A bad leader lacks follow-through in commitments. If a person in a leadership position talks about solutions, the expectation is that action will follow. If no action follows the mouth, the leader compromises his or her integrity.

At times, all of our integrity is compromised. We are all flawed humans in need of a Savior. During the times when we need extra help from God, it may mean taking a backseat on leading others, while we focus on regaining God's perspective in our own lives. God does not call and use perfect people. He calls the flawed and pours His perfect strength through us.

I have honestly expressed my flawed state, and how God has called me for such a time as this. God has called me to encourage others, and to make a difference in their lives. In II Corinthians 12:9-10, the Apostle Paul gave an account of the thorn he had in his flesh. He said he sought God three times to remove the thorn, but God's response to Paul was that His grace was sufficient for Him and His strength made perfect in weaknesses.

After that, Paul decided to thank God for his infirmities, since God said His strength operates in weak vessels. Paul did not complain or have a pity party, but begin to praise God for his weaknesses and thorns. He even said he took pleasure in his issues, and every difficulty he faced because he had finally come to the knowledge that when he was weak, then God was strong.

I acknowledge my broken, flawed, and gnarled state of life and all of my trials. And, like Paul, I still rise to live in such a way to show forth the power and glory of God.

As men and women of faith, we can overcome whatever has knocked us down. We can overcome and become victorious by depending on God every day to pick us up and empower us through His Word. We must accept what God has allowed in our lives, knowing it will all work together for our good.

No matter what we have been through, we can make it. We can do more than just "get by" because we are more than conquerors through Christ Jesus. The Bible says over and over again how powerful we are in Christ. The challenge is in recognizing the limitless power and access to God He has gifted to us. The gift of God is eternal life.

God has not taken back His Word. Every Word He has spoken is true, and it is the truth which makes us free. I recommend studying the Word of God to empower yourself and to begin believing in God and believing in the promises He has imputed to you.

It will not do us any good to have a bank account with a lot of money if we never withdraw from the account. God has deposited grace and mercy in our spiritual accounts. He has freely given us unlimited resources, but it is up to us to withdraw from it.

Application

I hope you get to know Jesus. If you do not already have a relationship with Him, now is the perfect opportunity to say a prayer and ask God to join you in your struggle. He is ready and willing to be the still small voice in your heart that speaks well of you and tells you everything is going to be alright.

Psalms 1:1-3 says, "Blessed is the man who walks not in the counsel of the ungodly, nor stands in the path of sinners, nor sits in the seat of the scornful; but his delight is in the law of the LORD, and in His Law he meditates day and night. He shall be like a tree planted by the rivers of water that brings forth its fruit in its season, whose leaf also shall not wither, and whatever he does shall prosper."

This scripture gives us two key ingredients to experience the peace of God. One is to love the Word of God, and second is to meditate on the Word day and night. Don't leave God out of the picture. Thinking on the Word of God has the power to transform our fallen nature into the nature of Jesus Christ.

Questions

1. Write in your journal about your greatest personal flaws. Maybe they are secret, and no one knows about them, or maybe they are thorns in your flesh everyone is aware of.

2. Do you recognize God calls the flawed? What is God calling you to do?

3. God's strength is made perfect in our weakness. What area of your life is weak? Write about how God will show His strength through your weaknesses.

chapter 13
Alright

Now to him who is able to do far more abundantly than all that we ask or think, according to the power at work within us, to him be glory in the church and in Christ Jesus throughout all generations, forever and ever. Amen.
Ephesians 3:20-21 ESV

When tragedy struck my life, I immediately tried to come up with a solution to solve the problem, instead of releasing the outcome to God. I begin to cry, worry, sulk, mourn, whine, and complain as if that was going to help solve the problem. Before I knew it, depression settled in, and I began to move slower and react with anger. I would rationalize my behavior saying, "It doesn't matter; I can't do anything about it."

In my eyes, I was justified in my sin. I felt sorry for myself with everything I had been through. I thought God was okay with my actions since I had had such a hard time in life, but He was not okay with sin. I pained the heart of God because I belonged to Him and I did not acknowledge Him in all of my ways. I only focused on my own needs.

As I continued doing what I wanted to do, the easier it was for me to drive by the church, to not read my Bible, and to convince myself it was okay to continue in sin. The longer I remained self-indulging, the further I away from God I became. I'm so glad God didn't allow me to reach the point of no return. Rather, He allowed me to come to my senses and make a turnaround.

The penalty for all of my sins had already been paid for on the cross. Did God still require me to repent? Yes. Did God want me to make Him Lord over every area of my life? Absolutely? Did God still love me, protect me, and take care of me? Yes!

God kept me because my position in Him never changed. My identity in Him never changed. Although I did not reflect the characteristics of my Father, I was still His child. God never moved. He never changed His mind about me. I moved away from God by acting out of character as a Child of the Highest, but His character did not budge. He remained faithful and true.

You may be wondering what happened after God gave me the victory over the hardship of my younger years. I thank God, I met a Christian man named James at church; the pastor and first lady introduced us. James and I married in 2001, and just celebrated our 16th anniversary! We serve in ministry at our church, where I am the Youth Pastor and James is a Deacon. The details of our beautiful love story are for another book, but I can say with confidence, "Thank you, Jesus, for the victory over my past!"

My victory did not come from I met my husband, James. My victory came through believing in Jesus Christ as Lord and Savior. 1 John 5:4 says, "For everyone who has been born of God overcomes the world. And this is the victory that has overcome the world—our faith." If we want to experience and gain victory, we have to believe Jesus is the Son of God.

Faith in Christ is what overcomes the world! Faith in the living Son of God, Jesus! Invite Him into your heart today and gain victory over sin! If you want to gain victory, get on the winning side. Turn away from sin, repent, and believe in Jesus Christ!

Lesson Learned

God showed me I was having a "Martha Moment" during my time away from Him. A Martha Moment is when we think it's all about us and it can't get done unless we do it. It's the idea, "I don't need God. I can handle my life."

Luke 10 recounts a conversation Jesus had with Martha about a struggle she was having being distracted and worried. To put it simply, Martha was stressed out! Her stress was evidence of a lack of faith in God.

Martha was so caught up in her own mess she forgot who she had invited into her home. Jesus was there! The man who turned water into wine, and fed over 5,000 people with two fish and five loaves of bread, was in her house!

The account, found in Luke 10:40, goes like this, "But Martha was distracted by the big dinner she was preparing. She came to Jesus and said, 'Lord, doesn't it seem unfair to you that my sister just sits here while I do all the work? Tell her to come and help me.'"

It's not that Martha should not have been preparing dinner, but it was the attitude she had while serving. Martha wanted to prepare for her guest, but in the process, she tried to control what Mary was doing. She then became lost in her feelings when Mary was content with sitting at the feet of Jesus learning from Him. Martha attempted to pour salt on Mary's choice to spend time with Jesus, but Mary was not the source of Martha's problem.

Verse 41 continues, "But the Lord said to her, 'My dear Martha, you are worried and upset over all these details! There is only one thing worth being concerned about. Mary has discovered it, and it will not be taken away from her.'"

Some of us are like Martha. We have forgotten we invited Jesus into our hearts. We fail to realize how powerful we are in the Holy Spirit, how we are more than conquerors, and that Christ lives in us. Where is the source of your issue? What makes you unhappy? What makes you angry? What causes you to complain?

Don't be a Martha and miss the presence of Jesus. It's time to find rest knowing Jesus can handle anything that comes our way. Martha did not have enough faith in Jesus to know everything would be alright. If she would just have taken a little time to stop and to see Him maybe she would not have gotten so tangled up with worrying about how it was going to turn out.

God loves us and does not desire for any of us to perish, but for all to repent and live eternal life. We must stop lying and rationalizing sin. The longer we hold out and tell God no, the easier and more satisfied and comfortable it is to live in sin.

Of course, the enemy will try to convince you to wait. We tell ourselves many lies that cause a delay in repentance such as, "YOLO—you only live once! You might as well enjoy while you can. Well, everybody is doing it so why can't I? Don't judge me! Only God can judge me. They're no better than me. I'm not hurting anybody. Well, at least I'm not on drugs. There's nothing wrong with it . . ." The irrational excuses we use to delay giving our all to God go on and on.

It is critical we make up our mind to finally surrender our hearts to God. Wavering back and forth on our commitment to surrender creates a spirit of carnality and a reprobate mind. In other words, when we resist the Lord the conscious mind becomes dull to the promptings of the Holy Spirit. The more we quench, or ignore, the Holy Spirit the harder it becomes harder to turn around.

I'm thankful I can say failure is not final. It was through my failure and my struggle I learned how powerless I am to live the Christian life in my own power. No one is exempt from the possibility of messing up big time. Nevertheless, His grace and mercy kept me through the good and the bad.

Truthfully, the solution to our problem is simple—always rely on God! God is saying, "Child, trust me! I got this!

While you're losing sleep trying to figure it out, I already worked it out." The promises of God are sure, and we can depend on what He has said. The righteousness of God is ours; we just have to put it on.

As God's children, He has given us dominion and authority. He calls us to reign as kings in life through Jesus Christ. God holds His people to a higher standard than unbelievers. We are royalty, and we need to recognize who we are and act like Children of the King!

Just as the Israelites had to conquest to make it to the Promised Land. We too have a conquest. We are a royal priesthood. We have to tear Satan's kingdom down and march into the spiritual Promised Land God has declared and decreed is ours.

Application

Read 1 John 5:1-5.

> *Everyone who believes that Jesus is the Christ has been born of God, and everyone who loves the Father loves whoever has been born of him. By this we know that we love the children of God, when we love God and obey his commandments. For this is the love of God, that we keep his commandments. And his commandments are not burdensome. For everyone who has been born of God overcomes the*

Chapter 13 • Alright

world. And this is the victory that has overcome the world—our faith. Who is it that overcomes the world except the one who believes that Jesus is the Son of God? (1 John 5:1-5 ESV)

When we think about victory the context of 1 John 5:1-5, we must also think about overcoming, the world—meaning the sinful nature. 1 John 4:4 says, "Little children, you are from God and have overcome them, for he who is in you is greater than he who is in the world."

To gain victory over the world, we must have Jesus in our hearts. Jesus tells us in John 3:3 we must be born again, or we will not see the Kingdom of Heaven. How do we become born again? That is the same question Nicodemus asked Jesus in John 3:4, "Nicodemus said to him, "How can a man be born when he is old? Can he enter a second time into his mother's womb and be born?"

"Jesus answered, "Truly, truly, I say to you, unless one is born of water and the Spirit, he cannot enter the kingdom of God. That which is born of the flesh is flesh, and that which is born of the Spirit is spirit" (John 3:5-6 ESV).

That's a strong statement from Jesus! Unless we are born of water and Spirit, we cannot enter the kingdom of God. Thankfully, the Bible tells us exactly how to be "born again" of water and Spirit.

First of all, we must believe in the one true God who put on flesh to die on the cross for our sins. His Name is Jesus.

Believing here is more than just agreeing that Jesus exists; believing is placing our trust in Him for forgiveness and eternal salvation.

2 Chronicles 16:9 says, "For the eyes of the Lord run to and fro throughout the whole earth to show Himself strong on behalf of those whose hearts are blameless toward Him." When we turn our hearts to Jesus and admit our weakness He will show Himself strong in our lives.

In the book of Acts, the early believers demonstrated what it meant to be born again of the water and the Spirit. "And Peter said to them, "Repent and be baptized every one of you in the name of Jesus Christ for the forgiveness of your sins, and you will receive the gift of the Holy Spirit."

When we repent of our sins—turn from our sins—and are baptized, the blood of Jesus washes away our sins. When we are born of the Spirit, the Spirit of God pricks our hearts to let us know when we have gone against God's commandments.

Join God's team and win! Victory is found in Christ alone! He alone conquered death; He defeated sin and death when he died on the cross for all of our sins, was buried for three days, and on the third day rose from the dead with all power in heaven and on the earth!

Questions

1. Have you experienced a time in your faith walk where you tried to take control over your life and stopped trusting in God? What were the lies you told yourself? What happened? What was the result of trying to live life on your terms instead of God's?

2. After that instance, did you give your life back to God through repentance? What happened? How did God show you His love remained?

3. Have you been born again of the water and the Spirit as Jesus commanded? How did turning your life over to God change your mindset and the way you approach life?

4. Take some time to write down your testimony. What has God exposed in your life? How does God want to use your story to bring Him glory? Share you story with at least one other person and continue to live your life as an overcomer, knowing God makes everything "ALRIGHT!"

about the author
Rev. Dr. Theresa Chatman

Rev. Dr. Theresa Chatman surrendered to God's call to spread the Gospel through ministry in February 2001. She was ordained as a Baptist minister under Bishop A. Tim Chatman in October 2002. She was appointed as youth overseer for Global Impact Ministries, and as a youth pastor under the leadership of Senior Pastor Bishop A. Tim Chatman, at Mt. Moriah Baptist Church in Ailey, Georgia.

In 2010, she completed a two-year program in Urban Youth Ministry from Fuller Theological Seminary Youth Institute, in Pasadena, California. Rev. Dr. Chatman has served as a youth worker for over 25 years. She is married to James A. Chatman, Sr. They have two adult children and one school-aged child.

She is an educator in the Dublin City School System and has worked in education for over 18 years. She attended Brewton Parker College where she obtained an Associates of Arts, Associate of Applied Science in Economics, and a Bachelor of Science in Early Childhood Education.

She later earned a Master's of Education in Special Education, Education Specialist, with a major in Teaching and Learning from Georgia Southern University. In August of 2015, she earned a Doctor of Philosophy with a major in Special Education Leadership from Capella University.

Rev. Dr. Chatman loves preaching and teaching the Word of God, and she spends her free time enjoying her family, reading, and writing. Much of the work she does in ministry involves youth ministry where she facilitates Bible Studies and plans and organizes events at Mt. Moriah Baptist Church.

She wrote *If It Had Not Been for the Lord* to empower women through sharing inspiration she gained through her life story of struggle, failure, and success.

Our Written Lives
book publishing services
www.OurWrittenLives.com

www.ingramcontent.com/pod-product-compliance
Lightning Source LLC
Chambersburg PA
CBIIW071739080526
44588CB00013B/2090